Red, White & Rosé

A Guide to Wines and Spirits

EDMUND PENNING-ROWSELL

Author of *The Wines of Bordeaux*

PAN BOOKS LTD   LONDON

First published in 1967 by PAN BOOKS LTD
33 Tothill Street London SW1
Second revised edition 1973

ISBN 0 330 237888

Consultant editor: E. Maxwell-Arnot
Design: Banks and Miles
Printed in the Netherlands by Drukkerij Van Boekhoven-Bosch
N.V., Utrecht

Photographs on pages 32, 81: Percy Hennell, pages 15, 39, 128: Ian
Williams, pages 52, 53: Colin Jones, page 93: Keystone Press Agen-
cy Ltd., page 102: Satour, Australian Wine Centre, cover and page
110: Banks and Miles.

Contents

Illustrations

Maps

Preface

The interest in and demand for wine has in the last few years been spreading enormously in this country. However, wine is not the easy matter that some publicists suggest. The variety of source and type, and the vagaries of vintage and handling, combine to make wine a fascinating but complex subject.

In the past this complexity, and all the supposed rigmarole of which-wines-with-what-food, the 'correct' glasses, and the 'right' temperature, has proved daunting to many. But the holidays abroad in the wine-drinking countries of millions of people have altered much of that. The desire to know more about wine is now widespread. Wine knowledge is even respectable, and to me seems socially desirable, for (to paraphrase that redoubtable French statesman Georges Clemenceau) wine is too important a matter to be left to the few.

Accordingly I willingly accepted an invitation from Bass Charrington Vintners to write the text of a popular guide to wines and spirits under their sponsorship. I was not least attracted to the project because, as one who has spent much of his life as a book publisher, I am aware that to produce a lavishly illustrated book on wine like this, for sale at a low price, is only possible with outside support. I have consequently availed myself of the facilities which such a large organisation is able to provide, to further my own knowledge. It is only fair to add that the opinions expressed are my own, and that the decisions as to which wines and spirits to mention have been mine alone; only in a minority of cases are they associated with the sponsors of this book.

Finally I would like to thank several professional members of the wine trade, without whose assistance no amateur can write about a subject complicated in character and inmensely varied: Baron Philippe de Rothschild and M. Philippe Cottin of Pauillac; M. Bertrand Mure, M. J. Dargent and Vicómte de la Giraudière of Rheims and Epernay; M. Hervé de Jarnac and Comte Alain de Pracontal of Cognac; M. Christian Cruse of Bordeaux; M. Alexis Lichine and Jacques Théo of Bordeaux; Mr. Charles Craig for his help on Scotch Whisky; Mr. William Wilson of Old Bushmills Distillery, and Mr. Michael O'Reilly of the Irish Whiskey Association for their help on Irish Whiskey; Mr. John Baker, Mr. John Symms, and Mr. Roger Holloway for making many helpful suggestions.

EDMUND PENNING-ROWSELL

5

WINE REGIONS
OF EUROPE

GERMANY

1

2

6

5

FRANCE

4

1

6

3

SWITZ

5

2

7

1

2

PORTUGAL

1

SPAIN

2

3

1

FRANCE   1 Alsace 2 Bordeaux
3 Burgundy
4 Champagne 5 Cognac
6 Loire 7 Rhône

ITALY   1 Tuscany 2 Piedmont
3 Verona 4 Orvieto
5 Marsala

GERMANY   1 Mosel 2 Rheingau
3 Rheinhesse 4 Franconia
5 Rheinpfalz- 6 Nahe

SPAIN   1 Jerez 2 Rioja 3 Valdepeñas

PORTUGAL   1 Oporto

Major wine-producing countries in colour
Lesser wine-producing countries named only

CZECHOSLOVAKIA

U.S.S.R.

4

AUSTRIA   HUNGARY

ROMANIA

3

YUGOSLAVIA

1

4

BULGARIA

ITALY

GREECE

5

Sicily

Crete

1 What wines and spirits are

It is a sobering thought that whereas in France the average annual consumption is 145 bottles per head of population, and in Italy 157 bottles, it is only seven in Britain – surpassed (with 12 bottles per head) even by the United States of America, which has, of course, the advantage of being a wine-growing country.

At least consumption is rising fast here, being treble what it was less than 10 years ago. Yet, although we have a long way to go, more and more wine is being drunk by more and more people. A generation or so ago, outside what might be called hereditary wine-drinking circles, wine was looked on with a certain suspicion. Those who wrote books on wine usually felt called upon to defend it against the claims of militant teetotallers, who, after all, scored a signal victory in making the USA 'dry' for nearly 15 years, between 1919 and 1933. That battle against teetotallers has now been won, owing partly no doubt to the fact that spirit drinking, as it was known even at the beginning of this century, has declined sharply. The amount of gin drunk in Britain now is about half what it was 70 years ago.

The other side of the picture is that wine has been discovered by many to be a very agreeable and not necessarily expensive accompaniment to food, whether at formal meals or at picnics or parties; and much of its appeal lies in the immense variety of wine – red, white and rosé, sweet and dry in many gradations, still and sparkling, beverage wines and fortified wines, as well as spirits and liqueurs. A wine merchant in Britain may well have between 500 and 1,000 different items on his list, and many others on call. In spite of this encouraging development of wine drinking, it remains true that there are still certain residual overtones of snobbery and extravagance associated with wine. To be known to drink wine regularly – perhaps with one's Sunday lunch – somehow puts one in an upper class and upper income bracket; and while it is considered a matter of course to spend, say, a £1 a week on cigarettes detrimental to health, to lay out £1 a week on wine can be thought to be wildly spendthrift. Fortunately this attitude is on the decline, and I hope to show in the course of this book that it is unreasonable.

On the other hand, in order to counteract the 'mystique' of wine, there has been a tendency to over-simplify the whole business and to suggest that 'there's nothing to it'; that all you need to know about wine is how to open the bottle. Aids to drinking, such as vintage charts, the correlation of wine and food and hints on serving wine are dismissed as pedantic snobbery or unnecessary complications. The implication is that if wine drinking appears to make any additional demands on people, they will be frightened off. Basically I believe this to be untrue. Millions of gardeners and anglers are quite willing to accept technical advice from books and magazines; and cookery books and recipes in journals are absorbed in enormous numbers. Why should people who are only too glad to know how to improve their pastry or their roses draw back at a few simple hints on getting the best out of their wine? It is, after all, owing to duty and other charges, not in this country a take-it-for-granted item on the weekly shopping list as it is in wine-growing countries. Wine at its cheapest here costs good money, and one might as well secure the best value from it. I believe that the 'there's-nothing-to-it' school of wine advocates both underrates the intelligence of the potential wine-drinking public and does no good to the cause which it supports.

True, it is not necessary to know anything about wine in order to drink it. There is no moral or physical obligation involved, except to know when to stop! No one should feel inferior because he or she cannot remember whether 1966 was 'a good year', or worry that a terrible solecism has been committed if claret is served with the ice cream. There are no justifiable social implications about wine drinking, no hideous pitfalls of social etiquette to be side-stepped.

Yet it is idle to pretend that the subject of wines and spirits is not a very large and complex one. The enormous variety of wines is evidence of that, not to mention the distinctions of vintages and age. But the parallel with gardening has some force. There is an enormous number of different varieties of roses and of primulas, and one can either buy a few standard varieties of plants or seeds from the local shop or supermarket, or one can deal with a specialist seedsman or visit a show of the Royal Horticultural Society. One can be perfectly happy with the locally obtained, more or less standardised, product and feel no inferiority on the subject. But there is no doubt that the more one feels inclined to go into the subject, to acquire a little basic botanical knowledge and to spend rather more money on one's hobby, the more one gets out of it and enjoys it.

So with wine drinking. One can drink, as it were, on several levels. There is the take-it-for-granted level to be found in wine-growing countries like France and Italy. Ordinary wine is on the table at every main meal, and it is drunk without comment, as water rather than beer is drunk in Britain. It is unthinkable to have a proper meal without wine, which may not cost much more than 6 or 7 pence or so a bottle anyway. Then there is the level where wine is something rather out of the ordinary, a minor luxury but not one to be taken too seriously. That is the position of many people in Britain today. The next stage is where discrimination and curiosity begin to intrude. It implies interest but not substantial outlay on wines. That is just about the level on which this book is written. Beyond that is the 'hobby' level, when wine is 'collected', when amateurs meet to discuss as well as to drink wines, and to organise tastings.

This last level, and I would be hypocritical if I did not admit to hoping that this little book would encourage some people to join it, must be distinguished from the wine snob level. Generally speaking, my experience is that people who are wine snobs are not very knowledgeable about wine. The wine manager of a well-known London hotel told me that a certain millionaire who frequented the place insisted on having a bottle of a certain celebrated and expensive brand of champagne by his side. It was a prestige symbol, not a token of knowledge. One of the reasons why the six or seven leading clarets of Bordeaux are so much more expensive than the others, is that they are bought by name rather than by tasting. Indeed, M. Alexis Lichine, the well-known wine expert and author of an excellent book on French wines, suggested to me that in many cases such wines were bought, privately or by hotels and restaurants, purely for prestige, and that 'no one ever draws a cork from one of these bottles'. This, of course, was an intentional exaggeration on his part, but one takes the point. This is the level not of wine expertise but of wine snobbery, and it does more harm to wine drinking than the assaults of total abstainers.

As wine is increasingly widely sold, the tendency for women to buy will grow, and before I proceed to discuss the different types of wines and spirits, I want to nail a frequent assumption that wine is a man's province, that 'the little woman' cannot be expected to fill her pretty little head with wine details, cannot be trusted to buy the stuff, and does not really know what she's drinking anyhow. Of course there is a basis in this, a relic of the days when a woman's place was in the home and perhaps in the kitchen, but not in the wine cellar. And there are still men, fighting the inroads of feminine advance, who will die in the last wine bin, before allowing their wives, sisters and girl friends to have even an arguable opinion on wine, let alone permit them to enter a wine merchant's, unless to admire their masculine expertise in juggling with vineyards and vintages. In fact it is my experience that when women give their minds to it, their judgements on wine are no less acute than on other matters. The only pity is that as yet there are not more of them, but the number is growing. And so it must in these times when wine, sold in the supermarket and off-licences, is increasingly brought home with the groceries. It is positively in the interest of men to see that their female relations and friends know about wine. So, 'Wine Women of the World Unite'; you have nothing to lose but your diffidence.

Types of wine and spirits

Since this book assumes interest but no knowledge, we must start by defining the terms we use. The definition of wine as used by the Wine and Spirit Association of Britain, which is similar to that of laws in wine-producing countries, is 'Wine is the alcoholic beverage obtained from the fermentation of the juice of freshly gathered grapes, the fermentation of which has been carried through in the district of its origin, and according to local tradition and practice'.

This excludes wines made from grape juice which is concentrated and then hydrated and fermented, as are so-called British Wines. It also excludes wines made from other fruits or from vegetables and flowers, such as apples, pears or parsnips. Fresh wine grapes are the prerequisites of wine as here defined.

The ways in which wines and spirits can be classified are numerous, but the most convenient way is by alcoholic strength. The low-strength wines are usually called beverage or table wines, and the high strength wines are known as fortified wines, since in nearly all cases their strength is created by the addition of spirit, usually brandy, to a beverage wine, as with port and sherry. Then come spirits, including liqueurs, which invariably have a spirit base, with the highest alcoholic strength.

Alcoholic strength

Low-strength beverage wines usually contain 10 or 12 per cent of alcohol, fortified wines have about 20 per cent, and the general run of spirits as retailed are about 40 per cent. For convenience and ease of memory one can say that fortified wines are twice as strong as beverage wines, and spirits twice as strong as fortified wines.

The exact alcoholic strength can be measured either by 'proof' standard or as a percentage of a liquid measure. Be warned, however, that British Commonwealth 'proof' does not tally with American proof, and that other countries use different measures.

The proof standard originated at least two hundred years ago and was based on the flash-point of gunpowder. As applied to spirits it means that at a stated temperature (51 degrees Fahrenheit) proof spirit contains 57 per cent alcohol by volume – comparable with the figures given above – or roughly $48\frac{1}{4}$ per cent by weight. The alternative measurement by weight is used in some countries, notably Germany, but the French and Italians reckon by volume. The Americans, using a round figure, make proof spirit to contain 50 per cent alcohol by volume, i.e. weaker than British proof.

It will be seen from this that the idea which some people have that proof equals pure or absolute alcohol is incorrect. In fact pure alcohol is $75°$ over proof.

The normal strength of brandy, whisky and gin as sold in Britain is $30°$ under proof, or, as it is more commonly put, $70°$ proof. This is the equivalent of 40 per cent alcohol, as will be stated on a French Cognac bottle. Until the First World War spirits were commonly sold in Britain at a higher strength than they are now. Whisky was $10°$ u.p., gin $17°$ u.p. and brandy and liqueurs $20°$ u.p. In the interest of 'the war effort' the Government ordained the lower strength which exists today. In the United States strengths are higher, so that most Scotch whisky is sold there at $75°$ proof, or $25°$ u.p., which on the American scale appears as $86°$ proof.

In Britain unblended malt whiskies are often sold at $75°$ or even $80°$ proof. As the duty is calculated on strength, such 'over-strength' whiskies will be dearer; each 5 degrees up attracts about 15p. more in duty. The high price of Green Chartreuse is partly accounted for by the fact that it is $95°$ proof.

Incidentally the American gallon contains only five normal bottles of wine, as against six in the British or Imperial gallon.

Wines

I do not propose to go into detailed descriptions of how wine is made, but a little basic information may be useful. The story obviously begins not in the fermenting vats but in the vineyard. Throughout the wine-growing world stricter regulations are being progressively applied by governments or officially backed organisations, to regulate and improve the standard of wine growing. In the fine wine areas the varieties of grape that may be used are frequently stipulated, as well as the density of planting and the limitation of output bearing the name of the particular vineyard. In France it is not permitted to plant a vineyard without permission, and in the European Economic Community there is an overall Wine Law. The lesser wine countries, anxious to dispose of their surpluses in expanding world markets, are following in the footsteps of the leading countries. There is a commonly held myth that wine was better 'in the good old days'. This is nonsense. One only has to read books on wine written a hundred years ago or less to realise the fearsome amount of falsification and illicit 'treatment' of wine that went on. Certainly there were great wines, but unhesitatingly I can say that the general level of wine is higher today than ever before, even though some fraud certainly still exists.

Red wine is, of course, made from black grapes, but it is possible to make white wine from black grapes too, so long as the black skins are removed before the fermentation, as happens in champagne. Most white wine is, however, made from white grapes. The methods are different. For red wine the grapes are crushed, with skins and sometimes stalks too, and then put into large fermenting vats, remaining there for one or two weeks until the fermentation is complete. The young wine is then drawn off into wooden casks to mature before bottling. White wine is made by pressing the grapes and then passing the juice without the skins into casks where it ferments. The size of the vats or casks is mainly determined by the need to keep reasonably constant temperatures during fermentation; for at too high a temperature the fermentation will stop, and so it will at too low a temperature. With the development of modern mass-production methods it is possible to use large temperature-controlled glass-lined, concrete or stainless-steel vats.

Rosé wine is produced by leaving the black skins in contact with the fermenting wine for a brief period, and then it is made like white wine. It is, of course, possible to produce a rosé by blending red and white wines, but this is a distinctly inferior procedure.

It is impossible to generalise about the length of time wines may lie in cask before being bottled. Some white wines are bottled six months after the vintage, others, like the great luscious Sauternes and rich Rhine wines, may lie in cask three, four or more years. Some red Beaujolais will be in bottle on Paris tables before its first Christmas, but most fine red wines are in cask for one-and-a-half to two-and-a-half years before being bottled. Clarets of a good vintage will be bottled two to two-and-a-half years after the harvest. The period needed for a wine to mature in bottle is even more variable. On the whole white wines develop in bottle less than red, but much depends on the type of wine and the vintage. A great claret may take twenty or more years 'to come round', but it can be excellent in a quarter of that time.

---

opposite: Wines being sampled for quality. The buyer 'noses' them, and also judges their colour and maturity.

Although every wine area makes wine each year, such wine may or may not be sold as the wine of that year. If it is, then the label on the bottle should state the date, and therefore the age, of that wine, and only that year's wine should be in the bottle.

If there is no such date, then it may be assumed either that the wine is a blend of several years' production, or that the grower merchant does not think that the date is important. A vintage date is not necessarily a guarantee of quality. In Bordeaux, for example, nearly all the vineyards sell every year part, at least, of their wine with a vintage date, and therefore one must consult a wine merchant as to the better vintages. In Spain an old date on a bottle of table wine may indicate the original year when a particular blend was started. In some other countries one suspects that the last popular vintage date is 'hung on' to the wines, and in others vintage dates are often thought superfluous.

It is sometimes argued that the introduction of scientific methods into viticulture and wine-making has 'ruined' wine. In fact, as with everything else, it is not science or the scientists that must be blamed but the abuses to which they may be subject. Too much sugar added to a red burgundy at the vintage will ruin the aroma and flavour of the wine, but in not-so-good vintages the addition of controlled amounts of sugar for the purpose of raising the alcoholic strength will turn an undrinkable wine into a drinkable one; but not into a great one. The clarity and stability of white wine owes much to filtering and the addition of sulphur. But the flavour can be filtered away with the impurities and the sulphur may overwhelm the aroma and taste. The bottling of wine is a more difficult operation than might be imagined; if there are 'bugs' in the bottle, the wine can turn into vinegar. It is also easy to have a secondary fermentation in the bottle, which may be all right if one is drinking sparkling wine but does not improve the taste if the burgundy in the bottle is nominally still. Science can certainly eradicate or lessen these difficulties. Altogether more care than ever before is being taken with wine and particularly about the inexpensive wines that most of us drink.

Beverage table wines

These are either red, white or rosé still wines. Although I have given their approximate strength as 10 or 12 per cent, in fact some German wines may be as low as 8 per cent and some red and white wines may be 14 per cent or more, notably Rhône wines. It is an illusion that rosé wines are necessarily less alcoholic because of their beguiling colour. They can be as alcoholic as any other beverage wines. These beverage wines are, as the name implies, the most suitable to drink with meals. The menfolk of Victorian novels were accustomed to drink half a pint of sherry with a chop, but this is not to be recommended with sherry as it is now produced!

Fortified wines

These are so called because they are strengthened by the addition of grape brandy or other spirit during or after the fermentation. When added during the fermentation the brandy stops or retards the action, leaving some residual unfermented sugar from the grapes in the wine. This is why port is basically a sweet wine, and why the drier sherries are usually less fortified than the rich styles. The basic fortified wines are port, sherry, madeira, malaga and marsala. In their various styles they are most suitable for drinking before, after and between meals.

The methods used for making fortified wines vary with the kinds of wine. The basic fact is that they are fortified with the addition of brandy, although there are some very fine dry sherries to which no brandy is added. The purpose of fortification is first to raise the alcoholic content, and secondly to stop the fermentation so as to keep the wine sweet. For some sherry the grapes are left to dry in the sun before pressing, and the brandy is added long after the fermentation period; but with port the brandy – made from local grape wine in all these regions – is added during the vintage. In the production of madeira, spirit made from locally distilled sugar cane is added during the vintage maturing process. Marsala, from Sicily, and malaga from Spain are two other celebrated fortified wines; with the first brandy is added during the fermentation, for the latter afterwards. Not all wine called malaga is fortified,

Sparkling wines

There are three common ways of making sparkling wines. The first, best and most expensive, is by inducing a secondary fermentation in the bottle, the *méthode champenoise*, since this is how champagne is made. The second is the *cuve close* way, in which the secondary fermentation is carried out in a sealed tank, and the wine is bottled with some sparkle still in it. This is much cheaper than the champagne method and is used for sparkling wines in France, Germany, Spain and elsewhere. A variant is to have the secondary fermentation in bottle, but then to blend the result in tanks, eliminating the longer champagne process. The third way is to inject carbon dioxide into a suitable wine and thus make it 'fizzy'. This fizz does not last long once the bottle is opened. The better sparkling wines are made from black and/or white grapes with considerable acidity, as good sparkling wine has to have a fair amount of acidity to hold it together.

Sparkling wines made by the traditional *méthode champenoise* are expensive chiefly because they require a great deal of handling and a fair amount of maturity if they are to be good. By a lengthy process the sediment is shaken down onto the cork of the bottle lying on its point. Then the neck of the bottle is usually frozen while the cork and fallen sediment are removed, and the 'liqueuring', which determines its sweetness, is added along with the permanent cork. This action is known as disgorging, and the champagne or other sparkling wine may be two or twenty or more years old before this is done, preparatory to the bottle leaving the original cellars on its way to the ultimate consumer.

Vermouth

It is not surprising that, with one or two exceptions like Noilly Prat of Marseilles, the Italians dominate the Vermouth business, because it was first produced commercially in Turin in 1757, and most of the big firms like Carpano, Cinzano, Cora, and Martini & Rossi have their headquarters there, but Gancia makes its Vermouth at Canelli. Vermouth is a blend of wines to which wormwood, some spirit, and infusions of herbs are added. The result is a liquor which is stronger in alcoholic strength than nearly all table wines, but less strong than the traditional fortified wines. There are two basic types, French and Italian, the former being considerably drier than the latter, the slightly bitter end-taste of Vermouth being largely attributable to the wormwood. As the French Vermouth makers usually also make a sweet variety and the Italian producers a dry one, the situation is complicated. To my mind the best of all Vermouths is Chambéry, produced in the French Savoy town of that name, on the other side of the Alps from Turin. It is aromatic and without the bitterness of French Vermouth or the sweetness of the Italian. Firms that produce it include Dolin, Moulin and Gaudin. Vermouth is also made in many other wine-producing countries.

Spirits

Spirits are high alcohol content distillates, produced by heating the liquid obtained either from fermented fruit, including grapes but also peaches, plums, etc., or grains, as in whisky and gin, or sugar, as in rum, or vegetables from which vodka can be produced. The heating concentrates the alcohol and extracts, to a smaller or greater degree, the water. Pure alcohol contains no water, but the brandy and whisky we drink contain, fortunately for our well-being, quite a lot of water, as measured by the proof already described. Nearly all spirits are double distilled. This applies to whisky as much as to brandy or eau-de-vie and applejack, but Irish whiskey is treble-distilled. The first, pre-distillation, stage is to produce a low-strength alcoholic liquid. For brandy it is a rather acid white wine, cider for Calvados, for whisky a beer-like liquid made from cereals. These are then concentrated by the first distillation to produce alcohol of approximately fortified wine strength or about 20 per cent by volume. The second distillation lifts the strength to 60 per cent (20° over proof) or more, when the vapourised spirit liquifies; on cooling it is run off into casks to mature. Not all of the spirit is usable in this second distillation and part of the skill of the job lies in eliminating the undesirable elements, which fortunately can be taken off at the beginning and the end of the distillation run. The essential maturing of any spirit takes place in the cask. For brandy this may be from five to twenty or more years, for whisky from three to perhaps twenty years. Whereas brandy will keep well in cask almost indefinitely, particularly if topped up to prevent oxidation – in Cognac I have tasted 1815 brandy – whisky may become woody after about twenty years in cask. Fine brandy is commonly put into new oak casks, whisky into old sherry or whisky casks. Spirits do not improve in bottle.

Brandy
This, at its best, is certainly the most distinguished of all spirits, although the devotees of single malt pot-still whiskies might dispute this. And the finest of brandies comes from the Cognac region of France – although there are advocates of Armagnac, also produced in France but rather further south and east of Cognac, in the Department of Gers. Grape brandy is, however, made in every other wine-producing country of the world, with varying success. Fruit brandies unsweetened by flavouring additions are often called eaux-de-vie, and they include Calvados (apples), Kirsch (cherries), Quetsch (plums), Framboise (raspberries) and apricot and peach brandies. Normally these are colourless, as arc all spirits after distillation. The colouring comes from the casks in which they are matured, or from added colouring such as caramel, which does not or should not affect the taste.

Scotch Whisky
Whisky is based on grain as brandy is based on grapes. By far the

greatest proportion of Scotch whisky on sale is blended. The heart and soul of the blend is provided by the malt whiskies made in the remote areas of Scotland in old-fashioned pot-stills from malted barley. Malt whisky alone is usually a somewhat heavy drink for ordinary occasions, so grain whisky, a true whisky made from maize and barley and distilled in a patent still (which is much more productive than a pot-still), is blended with malt whisky to make the lighter Scotch whisky blends that most of us know. There are four main districts in Scotland where malt whisky is distilled: the Highlands, the Lowlands, Islay and Campbeltown. Most of the patent-still grain distilleries are in the Lowlands. The proportion of the various whiskies used in the various blends is the blender's closest kept secret – although I expect their rivals have a pretty good idea! Generally speaking a blend will contain about 30-40 per cent malt to 60-70 per cent grain whisky. The de luxe blends may contain a rather higher proportion of malts or of older malts.

The epithet 'fascinating' is a hard-worked one in the commercial world, but there is no doubt that the production of whisky in particular is indeed fascinating, and for the following reasons. First, it varies in style from distillery to distillery, although they may be within sight of one another. Secondly, it is difficult to control this variation, however scientifically the whisky is made. Thirdly, the influence of local geology and water is an incalculable factor. Pot-stills vary in shape around the traditional onion theme and this certainly has some bearing on the style of whisky, but opinions differ as to why.

The first operation in a Scottish malt distillery is to treat the barley, first by germinating it, then by malting (drying) it in a kiln fired by coal and peat. This peat is an essential factor in the production of Scotch whisky.

The malted barley after being ground and mashed is called wort, and is ready to run off into the wash-backs where the 'sugar' in the wort is fermented by the addition of yeast in the same manner as beer, and then the resultant wash is distilled.

The first distillation in the wash-still produces a liquid of approximately fortified wine strength, about 20 per cent. This is distilled in the spirit or low-wine still for ten to twelve hours, during which the spirit comes off at an average of 25° over proof. These stills are normally situated in pairs and one can always tell the spirit still as it has a Crown padlock on it. The Excise authorities do not permit many drops of Scotch for domestic consumption to slip away dutyfree.

Like all other spirits, whisky is colourless when first distilled. It takes its colour initially from the oak casks – often sherry casks – in which it is matured for a minimum of three years. Indeed by British law neither malt nor grain spirit can be called whisky until it is three years old. Before then, in the eyes and records of HM Customs and Excise, it is just plain British spirit. Most blenders mature their malt whiskies considerably longer than that.

Although there is a small but growing public for 'single' malts (i.e. from one distillery only) outside the Highlands of Scotland, the traditional area of sale, only about 1 per cent of total malt whisky production is sold unblended. One or two of these malts are sold as bottled at the distillery: another sells its single malt in numbered bottles, and nearly all are obtainable around the local area of the distillery. Practically all malt whisky is used to give character to the lighter blended whisky that makes Scotch whisky the world famous drink it is.

A grain distillery is not without interest, but it is larger and more streamlined than a malt distillery.

The basic cereal for grain distilling is maize, which is softened in cooking to release the starch, but there will also be a good percentage of malted barley. After being cooked and mashed the cereals are now ready for the first fermentation in the fermenting vat or wash-back, the procedure here being the same as for malt whisky.

Distillation takes place in a Coffey or patent-still (named after its nineteenth-century inventor who was at one time Inspector-General of Excise in Dublin) which has the great advantage over the pot-still of permitting continuous production. It consists of two columns, the rectifier and the analyser.

The spirit is taken off at a strength appreciably higher than malt whisky, but it still retains in lighter form the flavours and characteristics of a true whisky. Both types are brought down in strength before being put into cask: usually to 11° over proof. Grain whisky does not improve much beyond five years old.

The real skill in producing our favourite brands of Scotch is in the blending, when up to 40 or so whiskies, the products of as many distilleries, may be employed to keep a standardised product. Once the blend is made it is usually run back into casks for six months or so to 'marry' before being bottled and sold.

Scotch whisky is one of the most important British exports. In 1972 the value of exported Scotch was £228 million, nearly 70 million proof gallons exported. Home consumption is less than 15 per cent of the total but contributes in duty annually nearly 200 million to the Government.

In recent years there has been a trend among Scotch drinkers to favour lighter whiskies. These are lighter in flavour, but alcoholically as strong as the others. They are particularly successful overseas.

Most whisky firms produce a *de luxe* whisky, a little but not greaty dearer than the standard blend. In my view, they are well worth the extra cost.

Irish Whiskey

Most Irish whiskey is pot-stilled, and is generally more smoky-flavoured than the blends of Scotch. Its aroma and flavour is distinct from Scotch. Usually it is a heavier whiskey with a certain oiliness about it that is attractive to some and less so to others.

Irish whiskey usually contains a much higher proportion of malt pot-stilled spirit and a lower one of grain than in the popular grain blends; generally about 80 per cent to 20 per cent, whereas in Scotland it may be as low as 30 per cent malt and 70 per cent grain. This contributes to the heavy, full flavour of Irish whiskey. On the other hand Irish pot-still whiskey is distilled three times in place of the usual twice. This tends to take out more of the impurities (a pejorative word, but it is these that give the flavour and it is the lack of them in gin and even more in vodka that makes them nearly 'neutral'). The result is a rather lighter whiskey at the end. Irish whiskey is traditionally sold at a rather older age than Scotch, for Eire insists on a three year minimum age, and it is sold at seven years old.

Apart from the extra distillation, Irish whiskey is made in exactly the same way as Scotch, with the barley malted over a peat, anthracite or coke fire and the soft water playing its part in the final result. I had the opportunity to visit Old Bushmills Distillery near the Giant's Causeway, established at least as early as 1784 – about forty years before the earliest licensed Scottish distilleries. The barley was stored above the malting floor in a curious wooden gallery running the whole length of the building. The only modern note was a couple of stainless steel wash-backs where the fermentation takes place over a period of from 52 to 70 hours. The actual copper stills have the same antique appearance as elsewhere, but they are now steam-heated rather than coal-fired. After the third distillation the strength may be as much as 50° over proof, instead of the 15° to 25° for a typical Scotch double distilled malt. It is, however, reduced to 11° over proof before being put into cask for maturing. Old Bushmills is less full-flavoured than some other Irish whiskeys I have sampled, and is much more like a Scotch whiskey.This is not altogether surprising as the manager, himself a Scot who had previously been at the fine Speyside distillery of Macallan, told me that he made 'a

Scotch whisky in Ireland'. The grain part of this blend comes from a distillery in Coleraine, which also produces a small amount of malt whiskey, as usual triple distilled. When I asked the reason for this triple distillation, the answer from both places was 'tradition'.

There are now only three active distilleries in all Ireland, the most important in the south being John Power of Dublin, where John Jameson whiskey is now distilled, and Cork Distilleries of Cork. Power and Jameson were both established in the later part of the eighteenth century, the latter is a nineteenth century consortium of local firms. These three firms in 1966 formed a joint company, Irish Distillers Ltd, to market their products.

Production of Irish whiskey is very small compared with Scotch, and currently is only about a million gallons a year, scarcely as much as the output of some of the larger Scottish malt distilleries, such as Tomatin and Glenfiddich. A Scottish grain distillery produces much more.

Old Bushmills makes two blends of whiskey, the Three Star – emulating the Cognac marking – and twelve-year-old Black Label. Jameson also market a liqueur whiskey with a minimum age of twelve years.

It is no reflection on other whiskies or other spirits to say that Scotch and Irish whiskies are probably the most honest spirit drink in the world, owing to the very strict Customs regulations. As already mentioned, no Scotch whisky can be sold as such until it is three years old. Then if a whisky bottle is labelled 'eight years old', it is a guarantee that the *youngest* whisky in the blend (and even if it is a single malt it will be a blend of whiskies of varying ages) is of that age; much of it may be ten, twelve or even more years older.

American Whiskey
This favours the 'e' reserved on this side of the Atlantic for the Irish, with whom perhaps it emigrated. It is made in patent-stills. Rye whiskey is made from malted rye or barley, while Bourbon originates from wheat or maize.

Gin
Gin is distilled from grain or molasses-based spirit to a very high alcoholic strength, about 160° proof. It then has little or no flavour or congenerics, but it is re-distilled in a pot-still to which some flavourings, the chief one being juniper berries, are added. Dutch gin has rather more taste, as the juniper berries and other flavouring agents are put in before the initial distillation; it is more 'oily'. The strength

of gin is then brought down to the normal commercial 70° proof and sold straight away in bottle, as there is no point in maturing it.

Rum

Most people associate the production of rum with the West Indies, but it can be and is made elsewhere in the world where sugar is grown, for example in South America and the USSR. Nevertheless the best rum comes from the Caribbean area, although the largest producer is the USA. So far as Britain is concerned nearly all the rum imported has come from the British territories in the area, notably Jamaica, Guyana, and Barbados. French rum from Martinique has, however, always been available, and Cuban rum too.

Rum is a by-product of the sugar industry. Most of it is made from molasses that have been fermented (sometimes with various fruit flavourings added). These are distilled occasionally in pot-stills, but more normally nowadays in patent-stills, and the varying styles are largely accounted for by the different methods of distillation, including the amount of esters and congenerics left in, and the strength at which the rum is distilled. The colour of rum mostly depends on

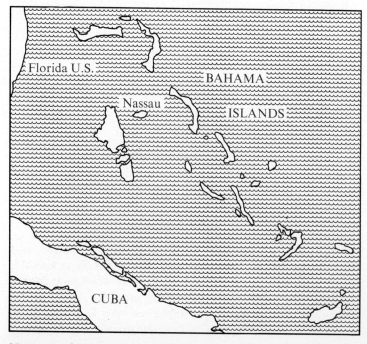

added colouring matter, particularly for the dark rums, although rum aged in oak for ten or more years will have a natural tinge of its own. Even then, such is the passion for standardisation, the colour will be equalised so that no suspicions may arise in the consumer's mind because the contents of any two bottles are not identical in colour.

There are basically three types of rum: the heavy dark rums from Jamaica and Demerara (Guyana), which are associated with Navy rum; the medium rums, from Trinidad, Haiti and Barbados; and the lighter rums from Cuba, Puerto Rico and the Bahamas. Martinique rum is on the heavy side; so is much American rum. However, all producers have been altering the style of some of their rums in order to meet the demand for lighter spirits. Moreover the largest 'light rum' firm, Bacardi, left Cuba in 1960, after the Castro revolution, and it has distilleries in Nassau, Puerto Rico, Mexico, Brazil and Spain; these produce Carta Blanca and three other styles.

In Britain the taste for rum was originally acquired by seafarers, who used the very powerful, full-bodied and pungent Demerara and Jamaica rums to keep out the cold. For many generations the Royal Navy had its traditional rum ration. Accordingly, demand gradually spread from the British ports such as Southampton, Liverpool and Glasgow, and the virtues of rum have generally been more appreciated in the pub than in the parlour. These powerful, sweetish rums are not to everyone's taste but the recent tendency towards lighter rums has encouraged their popularity both as a mixer in cocktails, and as a straight drink.

The really white rums are little or no more coloured than gin, and some have little more taste. Their real virtues are as mixers. However, there are superior types of so-called white rum, employing more matured spirits, and with a certain amount of colour acquired from ageing in cask. They are dry and can be drunk either neat or with soda and ice. I find these rums attractive neat. There are also rather fuller and sweeter light rums, called Carta Oro, as against Carta Blanca for the really white varieties, and these too have some character, but for connoisseurs there are the really old rums, which in this case means those with a cask age from ten to fifteen years. They are not oversweet and have a fine aroma. To my mind they make excellent after-dinner drinks, for although they have a certain sweetness from their sugar origin they are neither sticky nor pungent like the big-bodied rums, and they taste not unlike a slightly sweet but not unpleasant brandy. Among these fine old rums is Anejo made by Bacardi, San Martin, a Martinique rum, and Matusalem, said to have had fifteen years in wood, from Cuba.

Vodka

This is usually distilled from grain or potatoes, and is even more 'neutral' than gin. It is filtered through charcoal. It is a delusion that it has peculiarly lethal powers from which only leather-lined Russians are immune. Moreover, as produced in Britain it is usually sold at a much lower strength than Continental vodka, and slightly lower than domestic gin.

Marc

This potent drink is made from the residual tight-packed 'cake' of grape skins, stalks and pips left after a table wine has been made. Water is added, the whole is boiled, and a spirit is produced. Originally intended as a rough drink for vineyard workers, it is now, after maturing generally for five or six years, sold commercially. It is usually rather high in alcoholic strength and has a powerful flavour-cum-kick which is one of those acquired tastes that not everyone cares to acquire. Marc de Bourgogne, made from the residue of the Burgundy vintages, is often thought to be the best, but Marc de Champagne and Marc de Beaujolais have their vociferous supporters. The Italian Grappa is a marc.

Liqueurs

These are made either from brandy or neutral spirit. In some, like crème de menthe and curaçao, the flavouring matter of herbs and flowers is added before distillation; in others, such as cherry brandy, they are macerated for various periods in the spirit. In both cases blending follows. A method inferior to either is merely to flavour a spirit with essential oils. Liqueurs are always sweet, for they have added sugar, and they are usually drunk after meals as *digestifs*. The difference between them and eaux-de-vie, like kirsch, is that the latter are pure distillates and do not contain added flavouring. Incidentally 'liqueur' brandy is a misnomer, for brandy should not have any additional sweetening matter, although occasionally, but not too desirably, vanilla is added. The term 'liqueur brandy' is commonly used to denote a very fine old brandy, but in my view the epithet detracts from, rather than adds to, the implied quality of the brandy.

Bitters

These are spirits, flavoured by an infusion of herbs, diluted with water and coloured. Some are used to give a sharp, bitter taste to cocktails, others, like Campari, are popular as aperitifs, while Fernet Branca, also used in cocktails, is often regarded as a sovereign remedy for hangovers!

2 *Where wines and spirits come from*

FRANCE

I make no apologies for devoting much more space to some countries rather than others. The criterion has not been their quality but their availability outside their own country, and particularly in Britain, so France has the lion's share, and a whole chapter is needed to deal with its great variety. The average annual output of wine in France is 60 million hectolitres.*

Without a doubt France is the leading wine country of the world, not only on the score of quality but also of variety. More sparkling wine is produced in Germany, but who can doubt that champagne is the finest sparkling wine in the world? There are many imitation 'burgundies' throughout the world, from Spain to Australia, but they only underline the superiority of the original; and by common consent red bordeaux, or claret, is the finest dry red wine in the world. Moreover if any more bottles are needed to put on the scales to tip the balance, the brandy of Cognac so clearly leads the world, that its name is incorrectly invoked on brandy labels in many countries, including the USSR. To millions the name of the rather sleepy, not particularly distinguished little town in south-west France *is* brandy.

French wines can seem rather dear in comparison with the flood of wines now pouring into Britain from many other countries. Naturally, as with other things, the finest and most sought-after French wines are distinctly expensive. They are usually in short supply, and – this is not always remembered – this supply cannot normally be increased. The most famous white burgundy in the world is Montrachet, grown in a not very large vineyard on a hillside a few miles from Beaune. It is in the hands of a dozen proprietors, and it has been estimated that there are not much above 1250 cases – 16,000 bottles – available for sale annually on the world market. In Bordeaux the great châteaux vineyards are much larger, but nevertheless they are restricted, both by law and the limits of their workable land, in the amount that they can produce. An increase in productivity is ruled out, except by the results of modern techniques in reducing loss by disease in the vineyards, and by efficient operations in the cellars. Moreover if production were stepped up to any extent, it would certainly be at the expense of quality.

* A hectolitre is 22 gallons, and there are normally six bottles to the British gallon.

Wine and spirit map of France

NETHERLANDS

GERMAN

BELGIUM

ENGLISH CHANNEL

LUX

Seine

Rheims ●

Paris ●   Epernay ●

CHAMPAGNE   *Marne*   Strasbourg ●

Chablis ●   *Moselle*   ALSACE   Colmar ●

Loire   Nuits   *Saône*
St Georges ●

Nantes ●   Angers ●   Vouvray ●   Sancerre ●   Pouilly ●   Beaune ●

Saumur ●

VAL DE LOIRE   BOURGOGNE   SWIT.

FRANCE   Mâcon ●   *Rhône*

Cognac ●   ● Jarnac   CÔTES

COGNAC   Lyons ●   DU RHÔNE   ITAL'

BAY OF BISCAY   St Emilion ●   Bergerac ●   *Dordogne*   *Allier*   Tain l'Hermitage ●

Bordeaux ●   *Lot*

BORDEAUX   Cahors ●   *Garonne*   *Rhône*   CÔTES

Condom ●   Nîmes ●   Avignon ●   DE PROVENCE

ARMAGNAC   LANGUEDOC   Béziers ●

Narbonne ●

Limoux ●

ROUSSILLON
Banyuls ●

SPAIN

MEDITERRANEAN SEA

However, one does not have to drink Montrachet or Ch. Latour in order to enjoy fine French wine – even fine French burgundy or claret. The variety of the products of the French vineyards, scattered throughout the great majority of their ninety departments, is enormous. Many of these wines are minor, and drunk locally or regionally, and are little exported. Anyone going on holiday in the Jura, Savoy or the Pyrenees will find local wines, but I do not propose to enlarge on them here; nor on the wines grown in the enormous flat vineyards of the Midi, whence come most of the cheap wines to be bought in French grocery shops. There is nothing wrong with Midi wines, provided that they are well made, and the increasing quantities of inexpensive French wine to be found over here, often in litre and bigger bottles, are likely to come from the Midi.

Here I propose to deal with the main French wine areas, roughly from north to south, since that is the way many people on holiday will encounter them.

Appellation contrôlée

As more and more French wines, bottled at source, will bear these two words on the label, and as they are increasingly referred to in writings about French wines, a short description of their significance will help wine drinkers.

They represent a system of control over the growing of the grapes, the production of the wine, and to some extent the marketing from the superior wine-growing areas of France which began early in the present century with the delimiting of the specified wine areas, was slowly tightened up by succeeding legislation, and culminated in 1935 in a law which is operative today. As a result, for a wine to be entitled to an *appellation contrôlée* (AC) name on the label certain conditions have to be observed. It must be made from specified grapes only, and the vines from which these come are subject to regulations on density of planting and pruning, to reduce over-production at the expense of quality. The maximum quantity of wine per hectare is laid down, although it may be varied up or down according to the quality and quantity of a particular vintage. To administer this system an official body, the Institut National des Appellations d'Origine (INAO), was set up, and it has inspectors in all the AC areas. No AC wine can be moved from one cellar to another, or from a merchant to a retailer or a restaurant without an officially-stamped document; and there is a fraud squad to police the system.

Sometimes these areas are regional, such as the one that covers all

Alsace, or divided into districts or communes. There are 60 ACs covering the red and white wines of Bordeaux, the lowest being Bordeaux Rouge with a permitted maximum yield of 50 hectolitres per hectare, and a minimum alcoholic strength of 10 degrees, and the highest being one of the famous communes of the Médoc, such as Pauillac or St. Julien, for which the minimum strength must be 10.5 degrees and the crop no more than 40 hectolitres. In some areas, such as Burgundy, the top AC may apply to single vineyards; for example Chambertin or Montrachet. The system also covers sparkling wines and spirits.

It will be seen that an AC wine is not necessarily a very fine wine, but it is produced under stipulated conditions. About 15% of French wine production is regulated in this way. The system is not perfect, and evasion and fraud is by no means unknown with a product that is all too easy to falsify, particularly by juggling with the official paperwork. Although hitherto not accepted by British wine merchants, principally on the grounds of these frauds, the system must be accepted by us now as members of the European Economic Community (although fraud is practised in these member-countries too). It is fair to say that the AC system has helped to raise the standards of the better French wines.

Below the level of the AC wines, but above those of the French *vins ordinaires* is an intermediate rank of *Vin Délimité de Qualité Supérieure*. These too are regulated but subject to less strict controls. The majority lie in the southern part of France and represent about 5% of total French wine output. The label carries a stamp with the initials VDQS on it.

Champagne

As already mentioned, champagne is commonly made from black grapes and white grapes, roughly in the proportion of 70 to 30. Some champagne, however, is made entirely from white grapes, and this is known as Blanc de Blancs; the white grapes are mostly grown on a line of hills known as the Côte des Blancs. The black grapes give the body and firmness, the white grapes the softness and delicacy. Many people believe that champagne was 'discovered' in the late seventeenth century by Dom Pérignon, the Benedictine monk-cellarer of the Abbey of Hautvillers near Epernay. But what he did, it appears, was to discover that by inserting a cork into the bottle it was possible to preserve the bubbles of the champagne fermenting in the bottle, during the spring following the autumn vintage.

There is a syndicate or trade association of twenty-seven leading champagne houses, the Syndicat de Grandes Marques. The oldest of the houses is Ruinart of Rheims, which was founded in 1729. Dom Ruinart, said to have discovered earliest the virtues of blending, was a friend of Dom Pérignon, so both spiritually, and from a champagne point of view, Ruinart may be considered to have had unexceptionable antecedents! Other leading firms in Rheims include Veuve Clicquot, the three houses bearing the name Heidsieck, Krug, Lanson, Mumm, Pommery, Roederer and Taittinger. At Epernay are Mercier, Moët & Chandon, Perrier-Jouet and Pol Roger; while the leading house at Ay is Bollinger. There are many small firms making excellent champagne among them Boizel and Gratien & Meyer.

The degree of sweetness of champagne depends on the amount of cane-sugar solution in old champagne, which is added at the disgorging, when the frozen sediment, which has gradually been shaken down onto the temporary cork or stopper, is removed, and the permanent cork inserted. The type of wine is denoted by the description on the label, a description which varies from firm to firm. But there are certain basic descriptions. *Brut* or *Nature*, indicates an unsugared champagne, although, in fact, a small amount is normally included. Extra Dry, *Extra Sec* is usually a little sweeter; *Sec* is by no means usually dry, while *Demi-Sec* and *Doux* are really sweet.

The taste for dry champagne really started in Britain in the second half of the last century. Champagne was and still is frequently drunk with the sweet course. But port-drinking England would not think of giving up its after-dinner vintage port. So champagne was thought of in Britain much more as an aperitif or dinner wine, and therefore dryer. Even today champagne destined for Britain is often drier than that produced for domestic consumption in France. Britain is still the biggest export market for champagne, importing over 8 million bottles in 1972, though Italy may soon surpass it.

All houses offer non-vintage and vintage champagnes. The former is a blend of various vintages and contains younger champagnes. than will usually be found in a vintage wine, although that may also legally contain wines of other years than that on the label. Each firm tries to keep to a house style, particularly for its non-vintage blend, which all in all accounts for about 80 per cent of total champagne sales. Not very good champagne – sometimes referred to ironically in the wine trade as 'wedding champagne' – can taste green and acid, whereas it should taste fruity even when dry.

The decision whether to offer a champagne as a vintage wine is made by each particular firm, but it depends on the quality of the year and a little on the state of the market. Not every firm offers a vintage

One of the most picturesque vineyard châteaux is ancient Château d'Yquem in Sauternes (see page 52)

wine in every acceptable vintage year, but the best years recently have been 1959, 1961, 1964, 1966 and 1969. Vintage champagne is generally softer and better balanced than non-vintage, and often a little less fizzy – although this may not be a recommendation to some people. It is better for drinking through a meal than non-vintage, which perhaps is best for aperitifs – and surely the best of all aperitifs.

Pink or rosé champagne is made by leaving the skins of the black grapes with the pulp for a short time during the vintage or by adding a little red wine. Most of the champagne firms make small quantities of this, including Pommery, Roederer, Ruinart and others. As it is more difficult to make, it is generally, but not always, more expensive than the ordinary champagne. Its heyday is said to have been the Edwardian era when infatuated, not-too-intelligent young men liked to drink the stuff from chorus girls' slippers, a form of devotion which to me seems misplaced; however, better this than some priceless still wine finding its way into such a receptacle.

The champagne trade is certainly the best-organised section of the wine world in France. Its statistical information is superior to that of other areas, and the head of the information and publicity committee used to be M. Bertrand Mure of Ruinart, who provided me with some of the information here. I asked him what the professionals looked for in a champagne. He replied that there were three points to be considered. First the 'nose' should contain no 'off' flavour, such as of fermentation; it should be 'flowery'. Then the colour should never be dark, nor pink, nor so pale as almost to be 'white'. But it should be light in tint with small bubbles. Thirdly, the taste must contain no bad, extraneous flavour, as of decay or vinegar. It should not taste too 'winey', i.e. like a still wine, but fruity and fresh. The taste should not be 'short', i.e. it should continue while the wine is in the mouth and throat, and not disappear or thin out. Fruitiness is the first consideration, and the champagne should not be too acid.

Sooner or later one is bound to be asked about still champagne. It is a light, fresh, naturally rather thin wine, as might be expected from this northerly region for wine growing. It is a *petit vin* and the Champenois show their good sense by turning it into the finest sparkling wine in the world. Since the war, and the unfortunate injection of carbonic gas into a consignment sent, it is said, to Switzerland, its export is officially confined to EEC countries, in bottles only, and it must be sold as 'Vin Nature de Champagne'. In France it is very expensive for what it is, being not much less dear than the sparkling wine. The best may be sold under the commune names, such as Le Mesnil or Cramant. The red is light and usually from Bouzy or Verzenay. But still champagne is not a wine to seek out at great expenditure of time or money

How long does champagne last? In Rheims they suggest that a vintage champagne is at its best after ten years. But it can be excellent, if a little different in style, when much older than that. I have drunk 1914, 1911 and even 1898 vintages in Epernay. The secret of their long life was, in addition to their basic balance and quality, that the disgorging had taken place only just before consumption. In Champagne it is said that ten years is the optimum life of a disgorged champagne but there are exceptions. In fact in England I have drunk 1923 and 1928 champagne that had been disgorged over thirty years previously, but this was exceptional. As it ages champagne grows deeper in tint and fuller in flavour. When it gets too dark and heavy in taste, its virtue has departed.

Alsace

Drive east from Champagne and either turn south at Strasbourg or cross the very attractive, green, tree-covered Vosges, and you will arrive in Alsace. This charming wine-growing area has had a chequered career. Only when Alsace was returned to France after the First World War was wine-growing put on a proper basis.

Wine growers and merchants very sensibly decided to avoid the label complications of German wines and to do without single vine-yard names. They based their wines on the grapes from which they were made, cutting out the inferior varieties and relying almost entirely on what are called 'noble' grapes. The Second World War and the German occupation naturally dislocated Alsace wine production and its reputation suffered in many ways. Since the war, however, Alsace wines have greatly improved. They are fuller, less delicate than the German wines from the Moselle and Rhine, but the Alsatians like to say that in most cases they are more 'honest' wines. They are fermented right out, unlike many of the German wines, which are stopped short in order to preserve some unfermented sugar in the wine. The best of the Alsace wines are not sugared. Another advantage is that basically they are not expensive. Delightfully fragrant, they make delicious wines for summer drinking. Also they can be drunk very young, within two years or so of the vintage; but the fine wines keep well, and the really fine Alsace wines will keep for twenty or thirty years. Since the summer of 1972 all Alsace wines with A.C. must be bottled in the region.

The Alsace winefield stretches from north of Strasbourg to south of Colmar. There are two districts: Bas Rhin in the north and Haut Rhin in the south. From the latter comes the best wine.

Below are the grape names likely to be found on Alsace bottles – which are, incidentally, taller and thinner than German wine bottles, and contain 72 centilitres compared with the German 70 cl. The normal French and English table wine bottle contains 75 centilitres of wine, or $26^2/_3$ fluid ounces.

Riesling

The grapes from which the most distinguished wines are made. The Riesling produces a full but delicate aroma, and a full-flavoured but not normally very sweet wine.

Sylvaner
Much lighter wines come from this grape; they are inexpensive and ideal aperitif and picnic wines, and should be drunk young. Sylvaner production is very plentiful in the area.

Gewurztraminer
This highly aromatic wine with a soft yet fruity flavour is particularly popular in Alsace. *Gewurztraminer* is not a grape variety, but a particularly fruity, 'spicy' Traminer, but now all the Traminer wines are sold as Gewurztraminer. They tend to be fairly alcoholic, but their aroma and flavour make them as seductive in their way as a luscious Sauternes. *Gewurztraminers* tend to be among the most expensive Alsace wines.

Other grape names to be seen on Alsace wine bottles are Muscat, Tokay (a Pinot variety and nothing to do with the famous Hungarian wine), Pinot and Chasselas. Zwicker, Edelzwicker and Gentil indicate blended wines. There is some Pinot red wine too.

Best vintages
1953, 1955, 1957, 1959, 1961, 1962, 1964, 1966, 1967, 1971

Burgundy
As generally understood this is a large area physically, but one producing strictly limited quantities of wine, except in Southern Burgundy, which chiefly comprises Mâcon and Beaujolais. The other two areas are: Chablis, east of Auxerre and of the Autoroute du Sud, one of the main roads to the south of France; and the Côte d'Or proper. There is also the small Côte Chalonnaise.

Chablis is a world-known name, but its output is very small; and often, owing to frost, its crop is further reduced. Most of the chablis, so popular for drinking with fish dishes, is not genuine, and I am not referring only to the open imitations, such as Spanish 'Chablis', a perfectly palatable wine with little resemblance to the original, but to the French imitations. The grape used for chablis is the Pinot Chardonnay, here also known as the Beaunois.

The genuine article is a very dry, clean, fresh white wine, with an attractive 'dry', i.e. not full, sweet or heavy, aroma. Like other good white burgundies it should be distinctly pale in colour, and some people detect a hint of a green hue. Owing to the wide demand for the very limited quantities, if genuine it cannot be a cheap wine. The top ranking Chablis vineyards are known as Chablis Grand Cru, the next best as Chablis Premier Cru. The *grands crus* include Le Clos,

Valmur, Vaudésir and Grenouilles; *the premiers crus* Fourchaume, Montée de Tonnerre and Beugnons. Then follows just plain Chablis and, lowest of all, Petit Chablis. Sometimes one sees on wine merchants' lists the description 'Chablis Villages'. This has no official rating, but may consist of a blend of wines entitled to be called chablis with others similar in style from just outside the small area.

Côte d'Or

This consists of a long, basically south-easterly-facing range of hills running from the suburbs of Dijon to near the Saône at Chalon. It is divided into two: the Côte de Nuits, and the Côte de Beaune. The finest red wines tend to come from the former, the best whites almost exclusively from the latter. The problem of familiarising oneself with Burgundy is complicated by the fact that the leading wine villages on

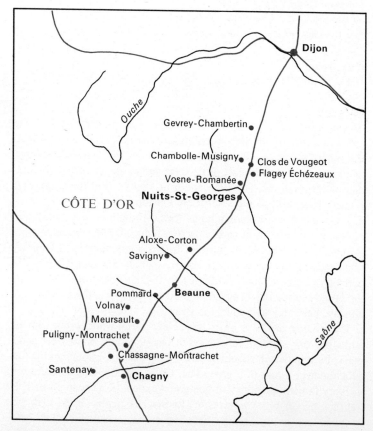

this long thin line – seldom much more than half a mile wide – have added to their own name that of the leading wine of the village. Gevrey, in 1847 was, I believe, the first to add the name of Chambertin onto its own. Chambolle attached to itself the celebrated name of Musigny in 1878, and Puligny added Montrachet a year later. This has proved good business for the minor growers of these villages, but it has been a headache ever since for amateur wine buyers. All that needs to be understood, however, is that the leading wines of each commune stand under their own names alone. For example in Gevrey there is Chambertin, Clos de Bèze, Latricières Chambertin, Charmes Chambertin, Mazis Chambertin and one or two more not commonly seen on labels. All the other growers have to use the village name Gevrey-Chambertin before the name of their own vineyard, such as Gevrey-Chambertin Lavaux; or from Chambolle village – Chambolle-Musigny.

A wine bearing a village name alone should be an excellent wine. If this is not always so, it may be owing either to poor cultivation or unskilled wine-making, to over-sugaring or to the blending in of other wines, which is the bane of Burgundy. The reason for this 'stretching' is the extremely small supplies of wines for which there is a world wine demand. Often less than 300,000 hectolitres of Côte d'Or wines are made in a year, whereas in Bordeaux the average is about 3,000,000.

The other problem of Burgundy is the multiplication of ownership in already small vineyards. The classic example is Clos de Vougeot, with its more than fifty proprietors, each determinedly making individual wine in his own way, good, bad and indifferent. Take into account also the uncertainty that prevails as to whether the wine in the bottle corresponds with the name on the label, and it will be understood why, in recent years, there has been a demand for domaine-bottled burgundy, that is, bottled by or for the owner on his property, thus giving the same guarantee of authenticity as château-bottling does in Bordeaux.

There are two views on this, for some maintain that few of the Burgundian growers, small proprietors nearly all of them, are equipped to bottle properly, and that the job is better done by the merchants in Beaune or Nuits. Others say that it is better to have the wine bottled in Britain, as it is much cheaper this way, and the British wine trade is very experienced in bottling wine. The opposite view has been taken among others by Alexis Lichine, who built up a demand for domaine-bottled burgundy in America, where nearly all wine is imported in bottle anyway. In order to overcome the problem of local bottling, he devised a portable bottling plant which visits the small proprietors, and bottles on the spot, thus making it possible to assert on the label that the wine is domaine-bottled.

However the trend towards burgundy being bottled in the zone of production is clear, and this includes beaujolais. It will not necessarilly be better thus and all that one can suggest in the way of advice is that red burgundy is *not* an unfortified kind of port, sweet and heavy, but a wine that is both full yet has a certain delicacy, with a fragant aroma that to me sometimes recalls wallflowers. It should neither smell nor taste sweet, and it need not look or taste strong and powerful enough for the corkscrew to stand up in the glass!

The famous grape used for the leading Côte d'Or red wines is the Pinot Noir; for the white wines Pinot Chardonnay. Lesser wines are made from the Gamay (red) and Aligoté (white) grapes. A Passe-Tout-Grains burgundy is from a blend of Gamay and Pinot Noir grapes.

If you are looking for burgundy on a list, it is better to pay a little more for a wine bearing a vineyard name than one with just a commune label. Below is a list of some of the best red vineyards in each of the villages of the Côte d'Or, set out in geographical order, running roughly south-west from Dijon to Santenay.

The important vineyards of the Côte de Nuits really begin at Fixin. There is also for all practical purposes a gap between Nuits St Georges at the end of the Côte de Nuits and the beginning of the Côte de Beaune at Aloxe-Corton, although wine is grown in some of the intermediate villages, such as Premeaux, Corgoloin and Ladoix-Serrigny. It may be assumed that the wines from these villages are sold under the names of their more famous neighbours. The starred vineyards* alone are allowed to be sold without the village prefix. Although the top wines are included, the selection of the others must be to some extent arbitrary, as there are a great many named vineyards. Most of the lesser wines are sold under the commune names only.

Red wines

Village	Vineyards	
Fixin	Clos de la Perrière	Clos le Chapitre
	Clos Napoléon	

Wine maturing in J. G. Thomson's vaults at Leith, with their famous fungus growth. It is being 'drawn off' with a 'valinche' for sampling.

Gevrey-Chambertin	Chambertin*	Clos de Bèze*
	Latricières Chambertin*	Mazis Chambertin*
	Charmes Chambertin*	Ruchottes Chambertin*
	Griotte Chambertin*	Mazoyères Chambertin*
	Chapelle Chambertin*	
	Clos St Jacques	Lavaux
	Combottes	Combe-aux-Moines
Morey	Clos de Tart*	Clos des Lambrays
	Clos St Denis*	Clos de la Roche*
	Les Bonnes Mares*	
	(a small part)	
Chambolle-Musigny	Musigny*	Bonnes Mares*
		(the majority)
	Charmes	Amoureuses
Vougeot	Clos Vougeot*	
Flagey-Echézeaux	Grands Echézeaux*	Echézeaux*
Vosne-Romanée	Romanée Conti*	La Romanée*
	La Tâche*	Richebourg*
	Romanée St Vivant*	
	Malconsorts	Suchots
	Beaux-Monts	Grande-Rue
Nuits St Georges	Saints Georges*	Cailles*
	Vaucrains*	Pruliers*
	Aux Murgers*	Aux Boudots
	Roncières	
Aloxe-Corton	Corton*	Corton Clos du Roi*
	Bressandes*	
	Languettes	Perrières
	Grèves	Maréchaudes
Pernand-Vergelesses	Basses Vergelesses	

Savigny-Les-Beaune	Aux Vergelesses	Marconnets
Beaune	Marconnets Fèves Clos de la Mousse Avaux Cent Vignes Toussaints Clos du Roi	Grèves Bressandes Clos des Mouches Vignes-Franches Teurons Perrières
Pommard	Epenots Pézerolles	Rugiens
Volnay	Caillerets Fremiers Clos des Chênes	Champans Angles
Monthelie	Champs-Fulliots	
Auxey-Duresses	Duresses	
Meursault	Santenots	Pièce-sous-le-Bois
Puligny-Montrachet	Cailleret	
Chassagne-Montrachet	Clos St Jean Boudriotte	Morgeots
Santenay	Gravières	

White burgundy of the area is almost entirely confined to the Côte de Beaune, but there are a few small white wine outcrops in the Côte de Nuits: at Clos de Vougeot, Chambolle-Musigny and in Nuits itself. In the Beaune region the best-known white wines come from four villages only: Aloxe-Corton, Meursault, Chassagne-Montrachet and Puligny-Montrachet. The last two are, as will be seen, linked with Montrachet, the greatest of all white burgundies, whose vineyard straddles the two. So does Bâtard Montrachet. The thing to look for in white burgundy is a fresh 'nose', a pale colour, and a fresh, non-sweet flavour. If the wine looks a bit golden in colour it is almost certainly heavy-tasting, oxidised, and past its best. The top wines like Montrachet, Chevalier Montrachet and Corton Charlemagne are expensive, from £5-£8 a bottle or more if French-bottled. It is usually worth while going for single vineyard wines, although a wine labelled just 'Meursault' from a reliable source can be excellent.

White wines		
Chambolle-Musigny	Musigny Blanc*	
Vougeot	Clos Vougeot Blanc*	
Nuits St Georges	Clos de l'Arlot	
Aloxe-Corton	Corton Charlemagne*	Corton
Beaune	Clos des Mouches	
Meursault	Perrières Charmes Goutte d'Or	Genevrières Poruzot Blagny
Puligny-Montrachet	Montrachet* Bâtard-Montrachet* Blagny-Blanc Garenne Pucelles	Chevalier Montrachet* Combettes Chaniots Referts
Chassagne-Montrachet	Montrachet* Criots Bâtard-Montrachet*	Bâtard-Montrachet*

Good vintages
1949, 1952, 1953, 1955, 1957, 1959, 1961, 1962, 1964, 1966, 1967, 1969, 1971, 1972

Southern Burgundy
This broadly comprises three areas. The small Côte Chalonnaise, which makes two attractive, rather light red wines, Mercurey and

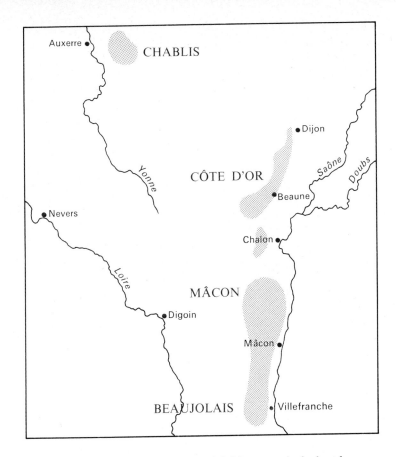

Givry, and one or two whites, of which Montagny is the best known. Then there is the Mâconnais, whence come many of the cheap red and white wines sold simply as Bourgogne Rouge or Bourgogne Blanc. They can be excellent or they can be very dull. But the chief wine of this district is Pouilly Fuissé, which at its best is one of the most delightful fine, but not outstanding, French dry white wines. The same criteria are to be applied as to the other white burgundies; and above all freshness and crispness. A recent new white Mâcon appellation is St. Véran, rather less good than Pouilly Fuissé.

South of Mâcon comes the long thin Beaujolais area, extending almost down to Lyons. These light wines have become highly popular in recent years, not only because they are light and attractive, but because they are inexpensive and can be drunk as young as any red wine of quality, i.e. within a year of the vintage. This has of course led to abuse, and there is certainly a good deal of beaujolais on the market that is either inferior, blended with other wines, or not beaujolais at all. True beaujolais always retains a certain astringency and sharpness, which distinguishes it from the more 'creamy' Côte d'Or wines. To buy a wine labelled simply Beaujolais may be a little hazardous, unless you know something about the source. 'Beaujolais Supérieur' merely indicates a rather higher alcoholic strength, 'Beaujolais Villages' means a wine from one of twenty or so named villages in the area. On top of these come the village names under which most of the best beaujolais is sold, for only a small number of individual growths sell their wines under their own vineyard label. Here are a list of the leading villages or wine areas:

Moulin-à-Vent (which stretches across parts of two village areas)	Chénas
	Côte de Brouilly and Brouilly
Fleurie	Chiroubles
Juliénas	St Amour
Morgon	

There is a little white beaujolais made on the border between Mâcon and Beaujolais, and it may be called either. Owners usually opt for the latter, as it has a more distinguished name, and secures a better price, but in fact it is not exceptional.

The Loire

The longest river in France is basically a white wine river, from the light, dry Muscadet grown in the region of Nantes, near the mouth, to the distinguished Pouilly Fumé and fragrant Sancerre, which are grown just upstream of that great bend of the river, when it turns from a northward course to a westward one. Muscadet is one of the cheaper white wines of France, suitable for summer picnics and for eating with the shell-fish of Brittany, but it can be disagreeably acid. The two up-river wines do not travel very well in cask as they are light in body. They often lose their freshness and life unless shipped in bottle. This naturally makes them more expensive, but they are delicious wines and quite unmatched elsewhere.

The Fumé part of Pouilly is not, as with Fuissé, a village name, but that of the grape, the Blanc Fumé. If made from the Chasselas grape then the local wine will be sold as Pouilly-sur-Loire. The wine is dry and not unlike chablis, but with a certain fullness of flavour that in the best known Pouilly Fumé, the La Doucette of Ch. du Nozet, sometimes suggests to me a very light Moselle. Sancerre is fuller, with a honey nose but a dry finish to the taste. British wine merchants usually have them bottled on the spot and imported thus. This puts them in the £1.40-£1.70 class, but they are delicious wines.

In between these two areas lie the large winefields of Anjou and Touraine. The most popular Anjou wines are, of course, the rosés. Agreeable, a shade sweeter than some other rosés, they are easy-to-drink wines without much pretension. The best are Cabernet Rosé, made from the Carbernet grape, but the finer Anjou and Saumur wines are the sweeter types from the Côteaux du Layon. These are not dear wines for their quality, and the finest of them all, Quarts de Chaume and Bonnezeaux are among the great sweet wines of France, and moderately priced at that. Owing to a good balance of acidity, they are often less luscious than Sauternes. Drier wines come from the Coteaux de la Loire, with Savennières as the best known village. There is dry white wine made near Saumur, but the speciality there is Sparkling Saumur. Made mostly in the traditional champagne way, it is certainly the best French sparkling wine after champagne and usually £1 or so cheaper. Owing to a certain snobbism about champagne it is under-rated in Britain.

A rival sparkling wine, but nearly always rather sweeter, is Vouvray from Touraine. It is also made as a still wine, but even then sometimes has a natural *pétillance*. Vouvray is quite a strong wine, although the alcoholic strength is masked by the sweetness. A similar wine made on the other side of the river is Montlouis. As elsewhere,

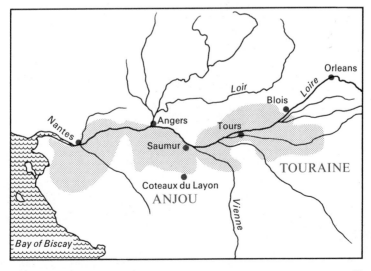

Bordeaux vineyards

	Sauternes
	Graves
	Entre Deux Mers
	Médoc
	St. Émilion
	Côtes de Blaye, Côtes de Bourg
	Pomerol
	Fronsac

Gironde

St. Émilion

Dordogne

Bordeaux

GIRONDE

Garonne

some drier wines are now produced under these names to meet contemporary taste.

South from Touraine come the best two red wines of the Loire: Chinon and Bourgueil. They are light, fragrant and inexpensive but not very significant, for all the connection of Chinon with that allegedly copious drinker, Rabelais. Just over the Saumur border is another red wine, Champigny, similarly light in style.

Bordeaux

This is the largest fine wine area of France, producing about $7\frac{1}{2}$ per cent of the total French wine production of around 60 million hectolitres. Large books have been devoted to Bordeaux wines, for they comprehend a wide and fascinating variety, from the great classed growths of the Médoc to the luscious, unchallenged Sauternes. A wine can only be called Bordeaux if it is grown in the Department of Gironde, and it has to satisfy other conditions of grape varieties, planting density and output, with an ascending rigour of control and limitation as the quality rises. There are five main areas: the Médoc, the Graves, Sauternes, St Emilion, and Pomerol. This division is to some extent arbitrary, for whereas Graves white wines are dry the Sauternes are very sweet, but they shade off into one another; this intermingling of styles is also true of St Emilions and Pomerols. There are also several minor areas producing excellent, inexpensive wines. These districts are, for red wines: Bourg, Blaye and Fronsac, all east of Bordeaux and on the right bank of the Gironde and Dordogne; for white they are Entre-Deux-Mers, Ste Croix du Mont and Loupiac. If one is looking for inexpensive Bordeaux, these names on a list or in a shop window should not be disregarded.

The 1855 classification

Médoc is the home of the sixty or so top wines known as the classed growths, or *crus classés*. They were classified at the time of an international exhibition in Paris in 1855, mostly on the basis of the prices they had fetched over many years on the Bordeaux market. There are five classes, and for many years this classification, reproduced on page 48, has caused endless controversy. For one thing, while Chx. Latour, Lafite and Margaux were put in the top class – along, illogically, with one red Graves, Ch. Haut Brion, from a district which does not figure anywhere else in the list – Mouton Rothschild was put at the top of the second rank. Since, even on the basis of price, Mouton has usually fetched prices higher than most of the other *premiers crus*, this grading was inconsistent. Whatever the reasons, the Rothschild proprietors of Mouton resented their classification ever since, and after many efforts at revision were given first-growth status in June 1973.

However, to those not in the know, a third, fourth and fifth class rating has implied a low-class wine, especially as far less distinguished wines in St Emilion and elsewhere proudly, if for many years unofficially, announced on their labels that they were first growths. The matter was brought to a head in 1955 when the St Emilions were officially classified, and a dozen leading wines were allowed provisionally to call themselves *'Premier Grand Cru Classé'*. Further, quite a number of the 1855 'aristocrats' are by no means making such good wines as heretofore. Some indeed are not making any wine at all. On the other hand some of the next rank of Médoc wines, known as *crus bourgeois*, are worthy of elevation. This is the 1855 Classification as amended now:

Red wines

First Growths
Ch. Lafite
Ch. Margaux
Ch. Latour
Ch. Mouton-Rothschild
Ch. Haut Brion

Second Growths
Ch. Rausan-Ségla
Ch. Rauzan-Gassies
Ch. Léoville-Las-Cases
Ch. Léoville-Poyferré
Ch. Léoville-Barton
Ch. Durfort-Vivens
Ch. Lascombes
Ch. Gruaud-Larose
Ch. Brane-Cantenac
Ch. Pichon-Longueville
Ch. Pichon-Longueville-Lalande
Ch. Ducru-Beaucaillou
Ch. Cos d'Estournel
Ch. Montrose

Third Growths
Ch. Kirwan
Ch. d'Issan
Ch. Lagrange
Ch. Langoa
Ch. Giscours
Ch. Malescot-Saint-Exupéry

Ch. Cantenac-Brown
Ch. Palmer
Ch. Grand La Lagune
Ch. Desmirail (now part of Palmer)
Ch. Calon-Ségur
Ch. Ferrière
Ch. Marquis d'Alesme-Becker
Ch. Boyd-Cantenac

Fourth Growths
Ch. Saint-Pierre-Sevaistre
Ch. Saint-Pierre-Bontemps
Ch. Branaire-Ducru
Ch. Talbot
Ch. Duhart-Milon
Ch. Pouget
Ch. La Tour-Carnet
Ch. Lafon-Rochet
Ch. Beychevelle
Ch. Le Prieuré
Ch. Marquis de Terme

Fifth Growths
Ch. Pontet-Canet
Ch. Batailley
Ch. Haut-Batailley
Ch. Grand-Puy-Lacoste
Ch. Grand-Puy-Ducasse
Ch. Lynch-Bages
Ch. Lynch-Moussas

Ch. Dauzac
Ch. Mouton-d'Armailhacq (now
   Mouton Baron Philippe)
Ch. du Tertre
Ch. Haut-Bages-Libéral
Ch. Pédesclaux
Ch. Belgrave
Ch. Camensac
Ch. Cos-Labory
Ch. Clerc-Milon
Ch. Croizet-Bages
Ch. Cantemerle

White Wines

Grand First Growths
Ch. d'Yquem

First Growths
Ch. La Tour-Blanche
Ch. Peyraguey { Clos Haut-Peyraguey / Lafaurie-Peyraguey }
Ch. Rayne-Vigneau
Ch. de Suduiraut
Ch. Coutet
Ch. Climens
Ch. Guiraud
Ch. Rieussec
Ch. Rabaud { Rabaud-Promis / Sigalas-Rabaud / Peixotto (no longer exists) }

Second Growths
Ch. de Myrat
Ch. Doisy { Doisy-Dubroca / Doisy-Daëne / Doisy-Védrines }
Ch. d'Arche (and d'Arche-Lafaurie)
Ch. Filhot
Ch. Broustet
Ch. Nairac
Ch. Caillou
Ch. Suau
Ch. de Malle
Ch. Romer
Ch. Lamothe { Lamothe-Bergey / Lamothe-Espagnet }

In 1959, Alexis Lichine, who then controlled two Medoc classed growths, Ch. Lascombes (now owned by Bass-Charrington Vintners) and Ch. Le Prieuré, startled Bordeaux by producing a re-classification of his own, reducing the classes to three, cutting out any numbered grades, and adding the leading red wines of Graves, St Emilion and Pomerol. In all they totalled 140 as against the original 60 or so. Broadly speaking Lichine's list makes sense, but of course it was by no means universally popular. Other suggestions followed, some official, others not. In 1972 the French government announced a new classification competition, in which classed growths and the best of the next level of estates throughout the Médoc wine district would be invited to take part. This will take some years. Meanwhile not all classed growths make good wine; even in good years the best of them may make disappointing wine. Also the non-classed growths can make as good and sometimes better wine than many of the classed growths. The best advice is to consult one's wine merchant, one's palate and one's pocket, in that order. Within the last few years nearly all the classed growths have insisted on château-bottling.

Médoc

This consists of the Haut Médoc, where the finer growths, including the classed growths, are situated, and the Médoc Maritime, the area towards the sea. The leading villages or communes are Pauillac, St Estèphe, St Julien, Margaux and Cantenac. Intertwined or adjacent to these are lesser villages, including Ludon, Labarde, Macau, St Laurent, Moulis, Soussans, Cussac, Cissac, Blanquefort and others, some of which number one or two classed growths in their midst. Some villages, such as Cantenac and Soussans, are allowed to use the name of a better-known commune, in these cases Margaux.

The style of wines in these communes varies considerably one from another, and even within them. Ch. Lafite is more delicate than that of the adjoining fuller flavoured Ch. Mouton Rothschild; yet both are in Pauillac. Broadly, the biggest wines come from Pauillac and St Estèphe, the most delicate from Margaux and Cantenac, with St Julien lying in between, as in fact it does physically.

It is impossible to make firm recommendations as to which are the best wine châteaux. Several châteaux, which made wonderful wines a generation or so ago, now produce rather ordinary wines, considering their status. Yet others are on the up-grade, including Ch. Palmer, Ch. Cantemerle, Ch. d'Issan, owned by the Cruse family of Bordeaux merchants, Ch. La Lagune, Ch. Ducru Beaucaillou and Ch. Brane Cantenac.

Many of these classed growths are now expensive, but there are a great many lesser Médocs known as *crus bourgeois,* which make excellent wine, and can sometimes outlive their social superiors.

What is claimed to be the best-selling claret in the world has its origin in Pauillac. This is Mouton Cadet, marketed by Baron Philippe de Rothschild's company. Branded wines i.e. blended wines with brand names, are always the subject of controversy, whether in Bordeaux, Burgundy or on the Rhine, whence Liebfraumilch stems. All the leading Bordeaux merchants sell their own brands; but Calvet's Ch. Tauzia and Barton et Guestier's Prince Noir excepted, they have achieved less popularity abroad than in France. Mouton Cadet is another exception. It began in 1933 when Ch. Mouton Rothschild, like all the other châteaux, had an enormous excess of the 1930, 1931 and 1932 vintages. I was told in Pauillac that its sale began to expand after the war, and it is now sold in 123 countries and territories; Britain is the largest market, but with the USA likely to overtake it. It is sold as a vintage wine, except in Sweden and Canada where the authorities discourage this, and although its territorial origins in the Bordeaux area are not disclosed, it apparently does always contain in its blend some amount of the two Rothschild class growths, particularly Mouton Baron Philippe. They also market two white wines, Agneau Blanc and Mouton Cadet Blanc, the former the sweeter of the two. Will branded table wines increase their sales at the expense of single vineyard products? The last attempt to do this in Britain failed but the trend is in that direction. It is perhaps significant that the biggest demand for Mouton Cadet and the better known brands of Liebfraumilch, like Blue Nun, Crown of Crowns and Hans Christof Wein, is in restaurants.

Graves

In Britain, Graves nearly always suggests a white wine, but in fact the best wines are red, led by Ch. Haut Brion, the sole red Graves in the 1855 classification. Most of these are clustered around or near Bordeaux, in the villages of Pessac, Léognan, and Martillac. The other leading growths include Ch. La Mission Haut Brion, Ch. Pape Clément, Ch. Haut Bailly, Domaine de Chevalier and Ch. Smith-Haut-Lafitte. Several of these make white wine also, and they are among the best dry white Bordeaux. Red Graves wines are usually rather lighter, less full-bodied than the Médocs but also very distinguished and fine.

White Graves is seldom as dry as white burgundy, but is for that reason popular with those who like a little fullness, even slight sweetness, in a wine. It is also inexpensive for a relatively fine wine. None of the imitations of white Graves approach it in flavour. There are a multitude of growths. The two best known are certainly Ch. Haut Brion Blanc and Domaine de Chevalier, but other celebrated growths include Ch. Laville Haut Brion, Ch. Olivier, and Ch. Carbonnieux.

As one goes upstream along the Garonne from Bordeaux the white wine becomes sweeter, through Cérons, Barsac and Sauternes on the left bank, and the small area of Loupiac and Ste Croix du Mont on the right bank, and also in the Entre-Deux-Mers district between the Garonne and the Dordogne.

Sauternes

The only real rivals as great wines to Sauternes, whose district includes Barsac and three other villages, are the luscious wines of the Rhine and, more rarely, the Moselle. The former are, with the exception of Ch. d'Yquem, very much less expensive, and even a fine Yquem, is nothing like so dear as the *trockenbeerenauslese* wines of Germany (see page 62). Yet since the last world war the sweet white wines of Bordeaux have suffered a loss in popularity. Owing to the fact that the finest of them are made from grapes shrivelled by what is known as *pourriture noble* (noble rot) and picked over a period of weeks, they cannot be as cheap as, say, Graves. At Ch. d'Yquem the vintagers go through the vineyard up to twelve times over a period of three months.

The Sauternes were classified in 1855, and the list is given on page 49. After Ch. d'Yquem the best wines are probably the two Barsacs, Chx. Climens and Coutet, and then Lafaurie-Peyraguey and Suduiraut. But nearly all are good, and very good value for the quality of their wines.

Pomerol and St Emilion

These two relatively small areas, lying about twenty miles to the east

of Bordeaux across the wide Dordogne, produce rather fuller-bodied wines than the Médoc, for the soil is richer. Their wines have several points to recommend them. First, with a few exceptions, they tend to be cheaper than the classed Médocs. Secondly, they mature earlier; thirdly, they have a certain roundness and richness, which appeals to people who may find the Graves and Médocs rather astringent, especially when young. For these reasons, in the last twenty years St Emilions and Pomerols have increased in popularity more than any other clarets, and to my mind they have produced some of the most attractive clarets of the post-war era. Pomerols are the fuller-flavoured wines of the two, and they come from a large number of often quite small and modest vineyards. The leading Pomerol is generally accepted to be Ch. Pétrus, with a reputation and small output that enables it to demand and receive the price of the Médoc first growths. Among others that often make good wine are Vieux Château Certan, Ch. Certan, Ch. La Conseillante, Ch. L'Evangile, Clos René, Ch. La Croix de Gay, Ch. l'Enclos, Ch. La Fleur Pétrus, Ch. Petit Village, Ch. Trotanoy, Ch. Gazin; but there are many others, and there is no official classification.

The leading wine of St Emilion is Ch. Cheval Blanc, whose exceptional fullness of flavour undoubtedly owes something to the fact that

Châteaux which give their names to famous wines may be gracious manors, like M. Alexis Lichine's Château Le Prieuré **(opposite)**, or large country houses, such as Château Lascombes **(left)**, now belonging to Bass-Charrington Vintners.

it adjoins Pomerol. The claim to primacy would be contested by Ch. Ausone, but, in my view, for many years it has not been as good as Cheval Blanc, although it is bracketed with the latter in the classification made in 1955. As in Pomerol, there are a large number of estates, and over seventy of them were included in this classification, some of them little known overseas. The leading growths include Chx. Figeac, La Gaffelière, Bel Air, Canon, Trottevieille, Beauregard, l'Angelus, Magdelaine, Pavie and Clos Fourtet, but this list is not anything like complete.

In the absence of detailed knowledge, it is often safe to buy wines from these two districts, as they may well be more acceptable for immediate drinking than the Médocs, which can be hard and thin, though unsurpassed at their best.

Lesser Areas
Those who like claret, but do not wish to face the cost of the more famous wines, should, as mentioned earlier, consider the lesser areas on the other side of the rivers from the Médoc – in Fronsac, Bourg and Blaye. Some excellent wines come from the often substantial, if not widely known, estates and village co-operatives of this agreeably hilly country overlooking the Dordogne and Gironde. Fronsac is near St Emilion, Bourg further downstream and Blaye opposite the middle of the Médoc. The wines are usually fruity, full-bodied and what the French call 'generous'. If they lack the subtlety and finesse of the greater clarets, they can develop plenty of character if allowed to mature for five or six years; often unfortunately they are not. The Blaye wines are the lightest of the three.

Bordeaux vintages since the war

Outstanding:	1945, 1947, 1953, 1959, 1961, 1966
Good:	1948, 1949, 1952, 1955, 1962, 1964, 1967, 1970, 1971
Above average:	1950, 1957, 1958, 1960

N.B. As in all cases some good wines were made in such off-years as 1946, 1951, 1954.

Rhône
More people probably pass the Rhône vineyards on their way south than pass any other major French wine area, but a smaller number visit them than elsewhere. In type the wines are often fuller, fruitier and of higher alcoholic strength than the burgundies, which they

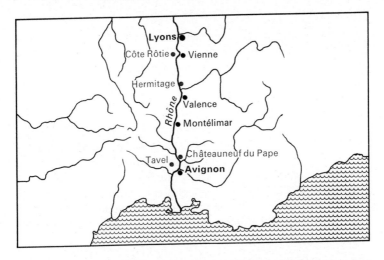

resemble, though lacking their balance. Grown in the warm but Mistral-affected river valley, these are almost southern wines – on the way to Italy. They are wines that need keeping, but in fact are usually drunk too young. The white wines could often be fresher, if better looked after and bottled more scientifically.

There are three main areas: Côte Rotie in the north, not far from Lyons; Hermitage; and Châteauneuf-du-Pape. The first are the lighter wines, and there is some dry white wine from Condrieu and Ch. Grillet, a three-acre vineyard with an *appellation contrôlée* of its own. Bottled in hock-style bottles, it is an interesting wine, with a nose reminiscent of an Alsace wine.

From Hermitage and associated Crozes-Hermitage come fuller red wines and some white wines which may be on the heavy side. Hermitage has always had a reputation for longevity; these days it seldom has the chance. Châteauneuf-du-Pape is one of those romantic wine names that has caught the public fancy. It is a big, bold wine and can be very good when it has had some bottle age; otherwise it may be rather coarse. A little white wine is made. Just west across the Rhône lies Tavel, whence comes the most famous French rosé wine; drier and with more character and body than most. The lesser reds are sold as Côtes du Rhône; the best known is probably Gigondas.

Good vintages
Similar to Burgundy, but with more good years than bad or indifferent.

Other French wine areas

Local wines may crop up anywhere south of the Loire, and even to its north. Few find their way abroad, although some have a reputation that is exported, and encourages wine merchants to import them. For example, the Jura wines, including red and rosé Arbois and the curious sherry-like *vins jaunes* of the Château-Chalon district; Jurançon, the usually, but not invariably, sweet white wine from the Pyrenees, which maintains its reputation largely because the French king Henri IV, who was born in Pau, esteemed it; Provence, whence come some excellent, second-line rosés, such as Château de Beaulieu and Ch. de Selle; Bergerac with its Monbazillac, a distinctly sweet white wine, and Ch. de Panisseau, a drier Dordogne wine. Cahors is the source of a deep red wine, sometimes referred to as black. There are many others, often proclaiming their local fame to passers-by.

Cognac

French brandy at its best is unequalled, and the finest comes from Cognac in the Charente region. Britain was probably its first foreign market, for when it was first produced commercially in the sixteenth century, it was shipped from La Rochelle in British ships. Still today, Britain is the largest foreign customer for cognac, and with a tradition of care and skill in its selection.

A good deal of myth surrounds cognac. So, to clear some of the ground, the only connection between Champagne and Champagne Cognac is that both come from the same French word, *champs* – field. Secondly there is strictly no such thing as a liqueur cognac, although the term is indiscriminately used to suggest a fine old brandy. As already mentioned, liqueur suggests sweetness, no recommendation for a brandy. Then, cognac, like other spirits, does not improve in bottle, so one may disregard the cobwebbed types occasionally to be met. Much the same applies to the alleged association of Napoleon with brandy. Colour is not usually a material consideration in appraising a brandy, for in most cases it is added to equalise the colouring naturally imparted from the oak casks in which it is matured; but better pale than dark. The traditional grading of stars and letters has largely lost its validity, as many firms have created their own gradings. This does not mean that a bottle labelled VSOP (Very Special Old Pale) is no better than a three-star, but one cannot compare brandies purely on that basis; and the old 'average age' which used to be ascribed to these grades is no longer accurate, if it ever was.

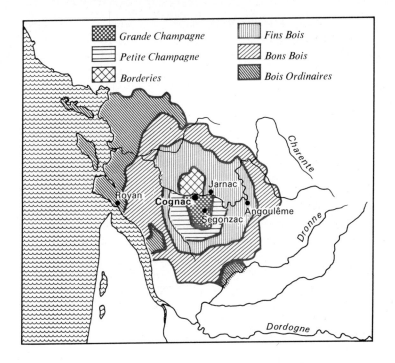

Genuine cognac comes from a number of strictly delimited areas, radiating, broadly speaking, from the centre at Cognac and Jarnac. The main districts are: Grande Champagne, Petite Champagne, Borderies, Fins Bois and Bons Bois. The Grande Champagne has more body but less finesse than the Petite. A cognac labelled Fine Champagne must come from these two small areas alone and contain at least 50 per cent Grande Champagne. The Borderies are powerful brandies, and then the others shade off into spirits of varying quality, those nearer the heart of the district being good, those on the outskirts not very distinguished, and tending to be coarse.

There is a good deal of nonsense talked about the age of cognacs. M. Hervé de Jarnac, the head of Salignac, told me that the age of the blend can be more important than the age of the constituents. For his firm's three- and five-star qualities the young brandies are blended as soon as possible after they are made and selected. They are then left to mature in wooden casks for three years; part at least of the blend will contain older brandies. Other firms do not make their blend until they require them for bottling, although of course time is allowed for the constituent brandies to 'marry' in the blending vats.

When it comes to the VSOP qualities, nearly all the reputable firms make it exclusively from Grande or Petite Champagne Cognacs. The finer cognacs will contain a proportion of those very old brandies which are the pride of their owners. In Hennessy's 'Paradise' cellars I have tasted authentic 1815 Grande Champagne, and other nineteenth-century vintages. They are kept topped up, until it is necessary to use smaller casks for the diminishing quantities. Contrary to what might be thought, these are strong alcoholically, about 75° proof, compared with the normal 70°, as sold. But it is not necessary to keep brandy as long as this, and it does not improve much, if at all, after thirty or forty years in wood. Forty years is generally accepted as the maximum time required for maturing; after that a cognac does not develop much, nor does it decline if topped up. The value of these old cognacs may be gauged by the fact that M. de Jarnac told me that whereas a cask of five-year old brandy would cost about £150 a twenty-year old could not be bought for less than £500. No less than 5 per cent per year has to be allowed for evaporation, although this decreases as the strength gradually diminishes. To keep the spirits from decreasing too much either in volume or strength they are put into large glass demi-johns. I have seen in the Hine cellars at Jarnac large demi-johns of 1875 brandy.

Although the public impression of Cognac is of large firms, selling well-known brands, in fact the Cognac area is one of small proprietors – 60,000 of them dividing 185,000 acres of vineyards. In the region there are 5,000 distilleries, of which about 3,000 work every year, starting when the new wine has completed its fermentation in November, and continuing until the following May. It takes eight barrels of wine to make one of brandy. The big firms do not own many estates, and some do not even own distilleries. There are only 198 professional distillers; the rest are *bouilleurs de cru,* distilling only their own produce. I owe these figures to M. de Jarnac of Salignac, which does have a distillery of its own.

Similarly, many of the 300 Cognac firms are family affairs. There are Hennessys in Cognac, and Hines in Jarnac, and the two directors of Salignac are descendants of the man who founded the firm in 1809.

Under existing regulations no cognac may be sold by the distiller in France with a vintage label if it is more than five years old. So no more vintage cognac will be seen, with one exception. There is in Britain an old but tenuous tradition of shipping one to two year old brandy and allowing it to mature in bond. When it comes down after about twenty years to a strength of 70° proof or less, without having to be 'broken down' with distilled water, it is bottled and sold. The colour of this 'early-landed' cognac is usually very pale, as it comes from the wood only, and it is exceptionally delicate. It is quite a different style from French-held cognac, and it is only fair to say that most French experts prefer the latter, as having more 'bite'. As it is scarcely profitable to hold brandy for twenty years, especially when it will evaporate, it is not surprising that early-landed cognac is rare – but to taste it is an experience to be sought.

Armagnac

This is the second brandy of France, and comes from the Gers region in south-west France. It is distinct from cognac not only in being distilled once instead of twice, but also in being distilled at much lower strength – about 10% over proof or even less, instead of an average of 22°. To my mind this produces a rather coarser brandy than the better cognacs, but by no means always inferior to some of the blends from the Charente. The best quality comes from the Bas-Armagnac, and there are those who loyally and loudly prefer it to cognac; *chacun à son petit verre!* Leading firms include Caussade, Janneau, Kressman and Montesquiou.

Marc

The various French regional marcs are popular with some people. All are very powerful, with a hard penetrating flavour that dominates all its manifestations, whether from Champagne, Burgundy or elsewhere. There are those who maintain that Marc de Bourgogne is the best, and the most palatable that I have drunk was a Marc de Meursault. But it is a case of one man's favourite marc being another man's near-poison.

Liqueurs

France is the home of nearly all the best liqueurs, of which there are an enormous number. Some have the apparent advertising advantage of having a monastic origin, presumably suggesting quality, a spiritual certificate of authenticity and non-toxic ingredients. These include Benedictine, Chartreuse and Vieille Cure. Among the secular liqueurs are Cointreau, Izarra, Grand Marnier, Crème de Menthe, and Cordial Médoc. I do not subscribe to the traditional view that the Green Chartreuse is superior to the Yellow; it is merely much stronger, and perhaps even a little drier, but I do not consider strength a merit in liqueurs, which are alleged to have digestive qualities.

Eaux-de-Vie

Alsace is the home of the fruit distillates from peaches, cherries, pears, plums and raspberries. I usually find that the cherry (Kirsch) and the pear (Poire William) are the best, although the raspberry (Framboise) is the most expensive, largely owing to the great amount of that fruit required to make a given amount of Framboise.

Calvados

The apple distillate of Normandy. It can be excellent, but is often either extraordinarily strong or excessively immature, probably both. It can provide an excellent alternative to brandy.

3 Other major European producers

This chapter deals with the four countries which, after France, in quality and/or quantity dominate the European and usually the world wine market. From the point of view of table wines, among these four countries Germany must take first place for quality.

GERMANY

The production of German wines is about 6 million hectolitres annually, although the 1970 figure was 9.9 million. This is infinitely smaller than in France, and only some 5 per cent is exported; yet Germany is from a quality point of view the second table wine country of Europe. Its best wines are white, as most of the wine areas lie too far north for fine red wine. For not only are German red wines sugared; they also quite legally contain a proportion of imported wine.

German wines are more conspicuously associated with the grapes from which they are made than French wines (except Alsace). So their grape names may appear on the label. The chief white varieties are the Riesling, the Sylvaner, and the Müller-Thurgau, which is a cross between the first two. The Riesling grows successfully only on stony or slatey soil, as in the Rheingau and Moselle. The wine is full-bodied and with a very fine aroma. The Sylvaner is the most widely employed vine in Germany, for it is easy to grow and produces a soft, light wine, less distinctive than the Riesling. The Müller-Thurgau is a very large producer, and ripens early – always a factor in northern climates. It is much used in the Rheinhesse and the Palatinate, as is the Sylvaner. The leading red wine grape is the Spätburgunder, which is the Pinot Noir of Burgundy.

Many of the difficulties of German wines for amateurs lie in the vast number of sites with different names – said to total 3,000 – the variations in quality on the same sites, and the intricacies of the labels.

The site names are usually less important than the village or commune names, and this cuts the problem down considerably. Some site names mean very little, as they may be used over an area far removed from the village from which they take their name, i.e. Niersteiner Domthal. The first thing is to remember some of the village names, as in Burgundy. The leading villages in the main areas are given below.

The quality and price variations within a given vineyard are certainly peculiar to Germany, with an overspill into Alsace. The lowest quality wines usually have just the village and site name, with the grape name, if it is from the prized Riesling or one or two other grapes: for example, Hochheimer Kirchenstück Riesling. Kirchenstück is one of more than a dozen vineyards in the village of Hochheim, from which comes the name hock, used only in Britain. One grade up in the scale would have *Spätlese* added to the label. Theoretically this means late-picked, and sometimes it may be true; otherwise it is a rather fuller, fruitier and usually sweeter variety of the original. With *Auslese* (selected) we should be in the presence of a very distinguished wine, for it is made from selected grapes or bunches. An *Auslese* should only be made in good years, and then the label would read 'Hochheimer Kirchenstück Riesling Auslese'. Really rare are the top two classes: *Beerenauslese*, made from selected very sweet grapes, and *Trockenbeerenauslese*, made from dried, raisiny grapes. Owing to the cost of producing wine from the liquorous but dried-up grapes, these last two wines are very expensive, often above £10 a bottle. Although opinions differ, in my view they are unequalled in quality; they are surely the finest sweet wines in the world, having a lusciousness combined with acidity that even the great Sauternes cannot match. They are possible only in exceptional years – once or twice in a decade.

Many of the problems of German wines for drinkers have lain in the multiplicity of vineyard or site (*lage*) names, and the intricacies of the label descriptions. To some extent these difficulties have been more apparent than real if one knows how to read a German wine label, for they are designed to help not to confuse the drinker.

However, the situation has been at least temporarily complicated by a new German Wine Law, passed in 1969, a revised one in operation from 1971, and the passage in 1970 of a European Economic Community Wine Law, which immediately had over-riding authority over any national wine law in the Community. However, many of the German provisions have remained and for the ordinary drinker there are three of these. First, the number of site names – allegedly 30,000 as mentioned above – has been reduced by about nine-tenths, for with certain exceptions no separate name is allowed unless the named vineyard is at least five hectares (12½ acres) in extent. So this very esoteric problem of knowing which are likely to be the best sites in each village or commune has been reduced, though it will remain of interest to keen amateurs, in the same way as the individual growths of Bordeaux or Burgundy are studied.

Secondly, some of the gradations of quality given on labels are no longer allowed. The most important to be cut out is *Naturwein* or *Naturrein*, meaning that the wine has not had sugar solution added. The old hierarchy of unsugared wines still remains. These include *Spätlese*, meaning late-picked, but in practice often only a rather fuller, sweeter wine than the normal one, *Auslese*, meaning selected, and only possible in fine years when the grapes in these very northerly wine areas are fully ripe, *Beerenauslese*, indicating selection by ripe berry and not merely by bunch, and *Trockenbeerenauslese*, a very luscious wine made from grapes that have been allowed to ripen on the vine to the point of drying up and becoming almost raisiny. While these categories remain under the new wine law, they are more specifically designated. For example, a *Spätlese* wine must have a stated minimum sugar-content.

However, in addition to these retained names, some of the rather fancy descriptions used by growers or merchants without any objective basis such as *Feine-Spätlese* or *Hoch-Feinste Auslese* are no longer allowed. In the past some growers have added the word Cabinet (or Kabinet). Originally this indicated a superior quality of wine reserved for the grower's own cellar or cabinet, and it was mostly used in the Rheingau, where the term started. Now it is brought into the new hierarchy, just below *Spätlese*.

Further, all the various ways of describing a wine bottled by a grower, in a merchants' cellars or elsewhere, have been simplified and other terms outlawed. Label descriptions such as *Originalabfüllung* (estate bottled), *Kellerabfüllung* (estate bottled), *Krescenz...* (from the estate of...) are no longer legal. Instead there are restricted forms of words only. Estate (grower)-bottled wine carries on the label '*Aus eigenem Lesegut – Eigene Abfüllung*' after the grower's name. This means the wine is of his own harvesting and bottled by him. If it is bottled by a merchant, the term for an estate wine is: '*Aus dem Lesegut ... A*', '*Abfüllung B*' (the merchant). An alternative for an estate wine is Erzeuger Abfüllung.

Much more revolutionary than these changes is the divison of all German wines into three categories: *Tischwein* (table wine), *Qualitätswein* (quality wine) and *Qualitätswein mit Prädikat* (a term impossible to render into English literally, but roughly meaning quality wine with honours). All quality wines have a sort of licence or *Prüfung* (testing) number on the label. The higher categories listed above are all quality wines, but now a Liebfraumilch, which is a blended Rhine wine from no specific location, may be described as a quality wine too. *Tischwein* cannot have a label name suggesting that it comes from a single place.

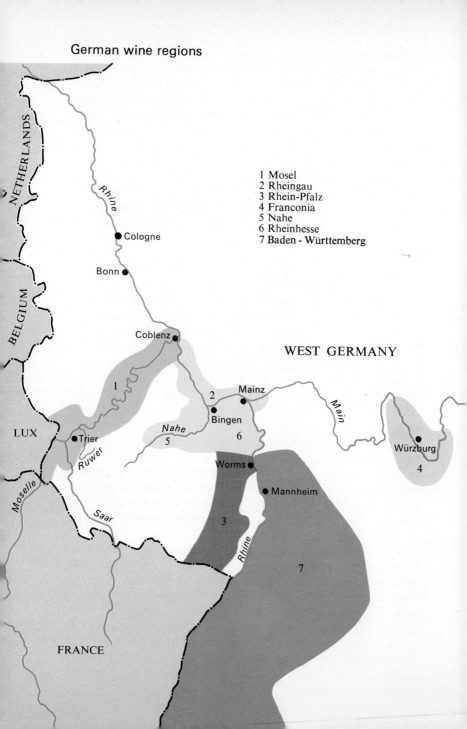

German wine regions

1 Mosel
2 Rheingau
3 Rhein-Pfalz
4 Franconia
5 Nahe
6 Rheinhesse
7 Baden - Württemberg

NETHERLANDS

BELGIUM

LUX

FRANCE

Rhine

Cologne

Bonn

Coblenz

WEST GERMANY

1

2

Mainz

Bingen

Nahe

5

6

Main

Trier

Ruwer

Worms

Würzburg

4

Moselle

Saar

Mannheim

3

Rhine

7

The variations that the EEC Wine Law have introduced concern such matters as the blending-in of a proportion of foreign wines without the German wine losing the right to a territorial description, and the amount of added sugar allowed. A transitional period of about 7 years will be permitted before all the regulations are applied.

Although intended for clarification, it cannot be denied that the new laws temporarily at least have added to the confusion of many amateurs, particularly since for some years to come older wines will carry the old-style label descriptions. It does remain true, however, that once the wine drinker understands the hierarchial system of German wine production, with its ascending level of quality being spelled out on the label, the whole matter does become rather easier, and henceforward the three main classes of wine will be indicated on the label too. Added to this, the growers will continue in many cases to put on the label the predominant grape from which this particular wine has been made – Riesling, Sylvaner (Silvaner in Franconia) etc. This means that at least 75% of the wine in question comes from the grape indicated. It may well be 100%.

The chief wine areas are associated with the Rhine and its tributaries, the Moselle, Nahe and the Main. The largest wine areas are associated with the Rhine. The Moselle wines are, however, often preferred for drinking with meals. The Nahe wines are midway between the two in style. Main (Franconian) wines tend to be dry.

The Rhine
On the Rhine are three districts: the Rheingau, Rheinhesse, and Pfalz or Palatinate. Their positions can be seen on the map on page 64. Of these three the Rheingau, with its unrivalled south-facing position on the great east-west bend of the river, produces the finest wines, mostly from the Riesling grape, the aristocrat of German white wine grapes. Rheinhesse produces a large quantity of what may be called middle-class wines. This is also true of the Palatinate, the largest of the three areas, but there also are some very fine, full-flavoured and generally sweet wines made in this district.

The main villages of the Rheingau, proceeding upstream are: Assmannshausen, Rüdesheim, Geisenheim, Johannisberg, Winkel, Hallgarten, Oestrich, Hattenheim, Erbach, Kiedrich, Eltville, Rauenthal, Martinsthal, Hochheim. Assmannshausen is the chief centre of red wine production, producing the best in Germany.

The chief wine centres of Rheinhesse are: Bingen, Ingelheim, Bodenheim, Nackenheim, Nierstein, Oppenheim, Dienheim.

Ingelheim is a red-wine producing area. From Worms in this district comes the name but not necessarily the wine labelled Liebfraumilch. Worms has a suburban vineyard named the Liebfrauenstift, surrounding a large church, the Liebfrauenkirch. But the wine from this vineyard is sold under its own name – Liebfrauenstift. Liebfraumilch's only legal qualification is that it shall be 'a Rhine wine of good quality and mild character'. Most of the better Liebfraumilch comes from the hinterland of Rheinhesse and the Palatinate: the origin of the less good is doubtful! Its success is the result of an attractive name, skilful blending and marketing, and the complexity of other German wine names. It is usually unexceptionable but rather dull, and sometimes oversweet, and lacking in acidity; and also for its quality rather expensive. It has a much larger sale outside than within Germany. Its chief merit is perhaps in serving to introduce many people to German wines.

The Palatinate, running along on the eastern slopes of the Haardt Mountains, is divided into three: Lower, Middle and Upper Haardt. The best wines come from the middle section; and from the villages in italics in the following list come some of the finest dessert-type wines in Germany: Herxheim, Freinsheim, Kallstadt, Bad Dürkheim, *Wachenheim*, *Forst*, *Deidesheim*, Niederkirchen, *Ruppertsberg*, Königsbach, Grimmeldingen, Mussbach, Neustadt.

From Freinsheim and Neustadt, which is the regional wine trade centre, come some not very exciting red wines.

The many minor wine villages of the Lower Haardt, which runs down to the French frontier, are not worth listing in full, but some sound wines may be found bearing one or other of the following village names. Hambach, Diedesfeld, St Martin, Maikammer, Edenkoben, Rhodt, Burrweiler.

Palatinate wines in general are rather fat, and often rather flabby, without the firmness and backbone of the Rheingaus. They are generally thought of in Britain as being sweet, but much dry Palatinate wine is drunk in Germany. Palatinate and Hessian wines are generally much less expensive than the Rheingaus.

The Moselle

This is the main wine tributary of the Rhine. It rises in the French Vosges mountains, passes through Luxembourg, where some minor but quite agreeable white wines are made, and then really gets into its wine stride near Trier, the 'wine capital' of the upper German Moselle. Vinously the river is divided into the Upper, Middle and Lower Moselle, with the fine wines coming from the Middle section, which begins in the neighbourhood of Thörnich and ends about Erden; the frontier shifts in accordance with the individual views and stocks of merchants, who may wish to claim marginal wines as Middle Moselles! The Upper and Lower Moselle wines usually lack sugar, and form the basis either of sparkling wine, called *Sekt*, or of the cheap, sugared wines to be seen at very low prices in German grocery shop windows. The lowness of the prices may partly be accounted for by the fact that up to 25 per cent sugared water may be added at the fermentation stage, except to wines in the superior grades and classifications.

However, there are two tributaries running into the Upper Moselle each side of Trier, which do produce good wines – the Saar and Ruwer. By law the names of these two small rivers have to appear on all Moselle wine labels used in Germany, and they must cause some confusion to the unitiated, for their wines are far less known, and in poor years are usually far too acid; then they are mostly made into *Sekt*. In fine years like '64, '66, '69 and '71 they are delicious, for they have a crispness which makes them very suitable with savoury food, as the richer Moselles are not. The Saar lies above Trier, and the chief villages roughly in geographical order running downstream are: Serrig, Saarburg, Ockfen, Ayl, Oberemmel, Wiltingen, Kanzem, Wawern.

Saarburg is the chief wine centre, Wiltingen the best known wine village. Here lies the most important vineyard, Scharzberg, but it does not add the village name to its own. A part of this vineyard is called Scharzhofberg.

The Ruwer is even smaller, and the chief villages are: Waldrach, Kasel, Eitelsbach, Mertesdorf. The last-named is known only for another vineyard which disdains to add the village name: Maximin Grünhaus, which is all in the hands of one proprietor, Von Schubert, and is a fine but expensive wine.

Trier itself is the home of a number of important institutions, some clerical, including the cathedral, and some lay, which own vineyards on the tributaries or on the main stream. There is only one significant wine village in the area, Avelsbach, whose wines are similar in style to those of the Saar and Ruwer, with which they are often confused. But there are a number of Trier wines, mostly drunk locally save in exceptional years.

The main villages of the Middle Moselle are, in order: Thörnich, Klüsserath, Leiwen, Trittenheim, Dhron, Piesport, Wintrich, Brauneberg, Lieser, Berncastel, Graach, Wehlen, Zeltingen, Erden, Uerzig.

As elsewhere, to give even a selection of site names is meaningless. To mention the celebrated Piesporter Goldtröpfchen signifies little; all depends on the grower and merchant. Here, as in the other main wine areas, there are proprietors of repute. They commonly own strips of vineyards in a number of the communes. Their names on a bottle bearing a good vintage year are the best guarantee of quality. The Lower Moselle produces the low-priced wines popular within Germany and mostly consumed there. The chief villages are Kröv, Traben, Trarbach, Enkirch, Zell.

Kröv (also spelt Cröv) is known for a wine named Nachtarsch, which is a generic and not a site name, and the ribald title proves amusing to its chiefly German consumers. Zell is celebrated for its 'black cat' wine – Zeller Schwarze Katz, an easy name to remember, and another generic wine of no great quality.

The Nahe
The Nahe enters the Rhine at Bingen, opposite the Rheingau, after pursuing a roughly north-easterly course from the Hünsruck Hills. The wines are heavier, fuller than Moselles, less full than the Rheingaus. Good wine is often produced in years of off-vintages elsewhere, such as 1963. The wine centre is Bad Kreuznach, a spa; and the main villages on, or lying back from, the river are: Schloss Böckelheim, Niederhausen, Norheim, Bad Münster, Kreuznach, Winzenheim, Bretzenheim, Roxheim.

A minor village producing minor wine is Rüdesheim, often confused with the far finer Rheingau town and wine district across the Rhine. The best-known site is Rosengarten, which has no parallel among the Rheingau sites.

Franconia
The Main is the largest of the Rhine tributaries, and it joins the river opposite Rheinhessen. Its principal wine area lies a long way upstream in Franconia, famous for Steinwein, whose flagon-shaped bottle, the bocksbeutel, has been copied as far afield as Australia and Portugal. Its use elsewhere in Germany is permitted only in a small area of Baden. The wines are usually dry, sometimes to the point of austerity, but in a great year like '59 or '67 they have a wonderful distinction of their own. To be good they have to be expensive, i.e. over £1.50 a bottle, for the cheaper Franconian wines strike me as dull and too dry. The main villages are Escherndorf, Rödelsee, Iphofen, Randersacker, Würzburg.

The Stein vineyard is near Würzburg and, with one or two neighbours, is the only growth legally permitted to call itself *Steinwein*, but the term is widely used to cover all Franconian wines.

Minor areas

The chief minor areas are in Baden and Württemberg, but wine is also made on an even more northerly Rhine tributary than the Moselle, the Ahr, and also near Lake Constance, known in Germany as the Bodensee. The best Baden wines are made in the Kaiserstuhl area, which faces Alsace across the Rhine plain. Others are the Markgräfler wines and those from Ortenau. The best known Ahr wines are red. The Württemberg wines are light and, like the products of all these minor areas, they are practically all drunk within Germany. Eastern Germany has an isolated vineyard on the river Elbe, near Meissen.

Good vintages

In the main areas the fine years are much the same throughout Germany. Recent fine years are '59, '64, '66, '69 and '71. Good but not great years were '61, '62, '67 and '70. These are generalisations only. For example, '59 was not particularly good in the Palatinate nor '64 in Franconia, while some excellent wines were made in '62 and '63 on the Nahe, and '67 was very fine in Franconia.

ITALY

Now generally surpassing France as the world's largest wine producer, with an annual output of 65-70 m. hectolitres, Italy is behind in quality. This is partly owing to its southern position, which inevitably leads to a deficiency in the wines of natural acidity and an excess of sugar, but until recently partly also to the generally backward, inefficient and inferior methods of viticulture and winemaking. In Italy laws to improve wine standards and eliminate fraud were passed as lately as 1963 and 1965; and conditions are improving.

These new laws were largely based on the French *appellation contrôlée* system of controlling quality wine production. So now there are three classes of Italian wine under the D.O.C. (*Denominazione di Origine Controllata*) system. The basic regional wines have a 'simple denomination' (*semplice*) which means that they do in fact come from the region named and have been made by traditional methods in that area. Much more important are the 'controlled' (*controllata*) regional wines. There are about 150 of these, although the number is gradually being extended as the Italian au-

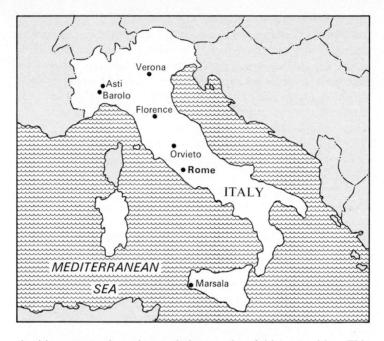

thorities accept other wines as being worthy of this recognition. This involves delimitation of area, the planting of officially registered grape varieties only, some restrictions on viticultural and wine making processes, and designation on the label of the wine being controlled. The top class is 'controlled and guaranteed' (*controllata e garantita*), just applied to Barolo and Bartaresco. It necessitates test tastings, local bottling and official numbered seals on the bottles. The word '*Classico*' may be added to the label in both controlled classes if the wine comes from an older producing area within a wider zone. The best-known of these is Chianti Classico, whose bottles bear a label with a black cock on a gold ground. But there are a number of neighbouring districts allowed to produce Chianti, each with its own individual neck-label.

Of course it will take Italian wines some time to achieve the desired results, and there are few large estates on the Bordeaux model, although the merchants may be vineyard owners too. However, in view of the need to export more than the present level of about 22% (ca. 13.5 million hectolitres) now sold abroad each year (of which about 6% is vermouth), the Italian authorities are making great efforts to raise standards to enable them to compete, particularly in Common Market countries.

Taking the main Italian wine districts from north to south, perhaps the leading area in the peninsula is Piedmont in the north-west. From here come full-bodied fruity wines, of which the leaders are Barolo, described by its producers as 'the king of wines', Gattinara and Grignolino. Barolo is a decidedly strong wine, needs to be at least four or five years old, and should be opened an hour or two in advance of drinking. Gattinara is a light, more elegant wine, while Grignolino is lighter still. In the second rank is Barbaresco, also full-bodied, while the basic Piedmont wine is Barbera, named after the grape. Another common wine is Barbacarlo.

Also from Piedmont comes Asti Spumante, named from the town of Asti, but mostly produced in the surrounding region. Made from the Muscat grape by the tank or *cuve close* method, referred to on page 17, it is distinctly sweet. This much quicker tank-method is said to be better for Muscat grapes than the champagne process, as it preserves the freshness of the wine. Of course this makes it much cheaper than champagne, and this is demonstrated by the fact that the biggest export market is France, which buys about $3\frac{1}{2}$ million bottles of the roughly 40 million produced and 15 million exported annually. A dry sparkling wine is also made by most of the firms, but as this cannot be called Asti Spumante, it is sold under various brand names such as Principe di Piedmonte or Contessa Rosa. Some is even made by the champagne method, notably by the old firm of Contratto. The leading Asti Spumante houses include Cinzano, Marchese di Barolo, Mirafiore, Contratto, Perlino and Gancia. The last-mentioned is the oldest and largest of them all. In the United Kingdom their wine is marketed as Gancia Spumante and not as Asti, as it is specially blended to suit the British market; it is drier, not being made exclusively from Muscat grapes.

The other leading north Italian wine areas are the Alto Adige, south of the Brenner Pass into Austria, the Trentino and the Veneto further south. The first of these largely produces red wine for export to the countries to its north. The best known of these is Lago di Caldaro, much of which is sold in Austria as Kalterersee. The leading red wine is, however, Santa Maddalena. A white Riesling wine is also made. The best-known Trentino wines are probably the red Merlot, Cabernet and Marzemino.

More important than these are the Veneto wines produced in the vicinity of Verona. The most famous is Valpolicella, a fruity wine, and the lighter Bardolino made near Lake Garda. This region also produces what is among the best Italian dry white wines – Soave. It can be fresh and firm, much-to-be-desired qualities in dry white wines, but often lacking in Italian so-called dry whites. There are some large concerns and co-operatives in this region. Among them are Bertani, Bolla and Lamberti, and there are large co-operatives at Soave, Monteforte and Bardolino.

From the Marches on the Adriatic coast comes one good dry white – Verdicchio, produced from the grape of that name.

Tuscany is the home of Chianti, hitherto the only Italian wine of international reputation. To date it has been associated with the straw-covered *fiaschi* but this may become less common, for there are labour problems in producing this straw covering; and also the shape is both awkward and expensive to pack and export. This is one reason why Chianti is, for its quality, often rather an expensive wine in Britain. More and more we are likely to see Chianti in normal-shaped, claret-style bottles. In the past much wine has passed for Chianti which was nothing of the sort, but under the new D.O.C. system control is much stricter and one should at least be able to rely on wine bottled in the region, which lies between Florence and Siena. Some large firms are involved in the Chianti trade, and they include Antinori, Frescobaldi, Ricasoli and Ruffino. There are also many good small firms in the area, the chief wine town of which is Grevé in the '*Classico*' district. Chianti is normally made from 80% red grapes and 20% white, and is usually matured for about three years in wood. It is no longer permitted to label the white wine of the area as Chianti. Two other good Tuscan wines are Brunello di Montalcino and Vin Nobile di Montepulciano.

The best known Umbrian wine is white Orvieto; it can be either dry, semi-sweet or sweet, but the dry is usually the best for drinking with food, though, as elsewhere in wine regions where some fairly sweet wine is produced, this latter goes down better on the spot than in our own colder climate. An excellent red wine is Torgiano Rubesco, produced near Perugia.

The celebrated wines made in the neighbourhood of Rome are known as the Castelli Romani, produced in the charming Alban hills to the south-east of the city. Of these much the most popular is Frascati, which is also produced in varying degrees of dryness and sweetness, but with a tendency towards the latter. Another familiar name is the white Colli Albani. The curiously named Est Est Est, from near Lake Bolsena, is probably better known in legend than from practical experience. It is white, and can be either dry or fairly sweet.

The further south one goes the fuller and more powerful the red wines tend to become, and the sweeter or 'riper' the whites.

From the Naples area comes the well-known Lacrima Christi, and there are red and white table wines known to visitors to Capri and Ischia. Aleatico is the red, sweet dessert wine of Apulia, and dessert wines are also made in Calabria.

In recent years Sicily, the largest Italian wine region, has made particular efforts to improve the reputation and the sale of its wines abroad. Marsala is of course the famous fortified wine, mentioned on page 17. The red wines tend to be on the robust, sometimes too powerful side, while the white wines are often rather heavy. Red wines I have liked at tastings have included red Castelvecchio from the Aurora co-operative at Salemi, the powerful red Etna Ciclope from vines grown on the seaward slopes of Mt. Etna, and the red and white Corvo wines from a vineyard near Palermo. The tawny-coloured, walnut-flavoured red Faro wines from near Messina have a reputation. A reliable brand is Regaleali from near Palermo.

These notes on Italian wines cannot do more than indicate some of the better-known names among a vast number of local wines often made from a mixture of different grapes. Visitors to Italy interested in the wines should visit the Enotica at Siena where 500 wines from all over the country may be tasted and bought. The problem of the Italians is to secure consistent wines of good quality and there is no reason why ever-stricter control should not achieve this in time.

Vermouth

Vermouth is Italy's contribution to the aperitif business, whether on its own or as a cocktail constituent. Details of its origin and production are given on page 18. Italian Vermouth is sweeter than French, although all the firms make a dry version, and a sweet white Vermouth too.

Spirits and Liqueurs

Italian brandy is not the equal of good cognac, but what other brandy outside France is? The best known name is Stock '84. The vintage date refers, not to the brandy, but to the date of the foundation of the firm. The national liqueur is certainly Strega, which is orange-flavoured. A speciality is Maraschino, made from cherries, and produced in the Venetian province, although originally it came from Dalmatia.

Italian vintages

These are of minor importance, as in all Mediterranean wine-growing countries, and the vintage labels are not always reliable.

PORTUGAL

In the last century and even earlier Portuguese table wines were commonly imported into Britain, as may be seen on old wine labels bearing the names Bucellas and Lisbon. Then, when the prohibitive 'political' duty on French wines was lowered, and finally placed on the same level as for other imported table wines by Mr. Gladstone in 1860, the table wines of Portugal, as of other countries, could not compete, and for many years Portugal on the wine list meant port. However, with the growth of wine drinking in recent years, Portuguese table wines have been regaining some of their old popularity, as they can now undercut the cheaper French wines. Sensibly, in my view, they have not tried to utilise French wine names, but have either been sold under regional names, like Dão, or under brand names, or both.

Wine is grown the length of Portugal, but there are three main areas: the Minho in the north; the Douro where the wine for port is grown; and the Dão.

The Minho is celebrated for its *Vinhos Verdes*, young, low-strength wines which still retain some of their fermentation sparkle. These may be red, white or rosé, and on the spot they are most

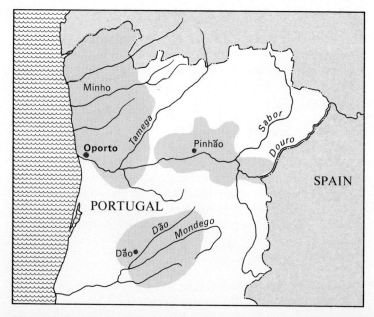

refreshing. One or two are imported into England, including Lagosta, white and rosé, and Casal Garcia, white. Mateus Rosé is not a *vinho verde*, but a slightly sparkling rosé. All these wines need serving well chilled as otherwise they tend to be over-sweet.

The wine which becomes port is grown on the bare, savage-looking slopes of the upper Douro valley and is then brought down that river to Vila Nova de Gaia, on the opposite bank of the Douro to Oporto. But the wine is made at its original source; then brandy, produced from distilled Portuguese wine, is added to the quantity of about 25 per cent. The addition of the brandy stops the fermentation, and so the wine retains a proportion of the natural sugar which otherwise would be turned into alcohol.

There are basically two types – port aged in wood and port aged in bottle. Port aged in wood and then bottled for more or less immediate drinking is a blended wine. The cask, in which it is matured, is periodically 'refreshed', mostly by younger wine and some additional brandy, but occasionally from other old tawny ports. The least expensive type of port is called ruby, a full-coloured wine with a good deal of sweetness. If the wine is left longer in wood it will gradually lose its red colour and become browner, as happens also with old table wines. Hence the name tawny. Tawny is drier than ruby port, and it can be very old indeed. At a luncheon held in London to celebrate the 150th anniversary of the Battle of Waterloo the firm of Cockburn gave the guests a tawny port which was guaranteed to be at least fifty years old. It had great distinction and flavour.

Port aged in bottle is generally what is known as vintage port. It forms a small part of port production and it is offered only in good years *and* when the Oporto shippers feel that they can successfully sell a vintage port, for which the market is limited and does not extend much beyond Britain, Belgium and Scandinavia; but chiefly in Britain.

If the shipper is satisfied about the quality of his port and its saleability he will then 'declare' a vintage. He will probably not be alone in this, but there is by no means unanimous agreement on the matter, and the decision is the shipper's own. Cockburn declared no vintage between 1912 and 1927. Some firms declared 1934, others 1935. Both shippers and the more senior generation of vintage port drinkers are still arguing which is, or was, the better year. Hardly anyone declared 1931 for, although the vintage was outstanding, the world was in the middle of the Great Slump. Yet Quinta do Noval 1931 is generally accepted as one of the great ports of the century. Even if the market could stand a series of vintage years, the Oporto merchants could not cream off the finest wines year after year, as these are needed for their standard blends.

Vintage port is landed in Britain, and elsewhere, two years after the vintage, and is normally bottled by, or soon after, the end of that second year. It then needs anything from twelve to twenty years in bottle before reaching its best. It is likely to stay at this point until about thirty years old, and may then decline, but this depends on the vintage, the quality of the bottling, and how the wine has been kept. Vintage port is increasingly bottled in Oporto, but unless it is shipped fairly soon afterwards, it is not reckoned to mature so well in the hot Portuguese climate.

Good vintages
1927, 1931, 1934, 1935, 1945, 1947, 1948, 1950, 1955, 1958, 1960, 1963, 1966, 1967 and 1970.

There are one or two other varieties of port. *Crusted port* is a blend of fine quality wines of more than one vintage and aged in bottle in the same way as vintage port, although it may be ready to drink rather earlier. It is also less expensive. *Late-bottled vintage port* is largely self-explanatory. Having had more time in wood, where it will mature more rapidly, it need not be kept long in bottle. It lacks the quality of vintage port, but as this is both rare and expensive, LBV makes a reasonable alternative. *White port* is made from white grapes. Formerly somewhat looked down on by true port devotees, it is now produced by the port trade as an alternative aperitif to sherry. It is sweeter than dry sherry, but, served chilled on a warm day, is very acceptable. Sandeman's Porto Branco is one example.

Sound table wines also come from the Douro valley, with the sweeter white wines produced quite near, but outside the delimited port area. There are also some sweet red wines from this area. Both are generally sold under brand names, as are the drier white wines lower down the Douro valley. The better branded red wines will have had three years in wood before shipment.

Dão, the third important Portuguese wine area, lies roughly to the south-east of Oporto, and from here come the best table wines, particularly the red. When young they tend to be rather powerful, but after ten years in bottle they can be excellent, with more body than most clarets but less full than the majority of burgundies. These are likely to bear vintage labels, whereas the cheaper, younger wines are probably blends.

Further south in Portugal are a number of interesting red and white wines, mostly not exported, such as Bucellas, a dry white wine that used to be sold in Britain in the last century as 'Portuguese Hock'; Colares, a red wine produced in sandy vineyards near the sea, and requiring considerable bottle age; Moscatel de Setúbal, a rich dessert wine; Palmela, another sweet wine; Periquita, a full-bodied branded red wine, of considerable merit in its class.

Portuguese brandy can be agreeable, but is not much seen in Britain.

Vintages

Vintages are unimportant except as an indication of age in a red wine. As in Spain the *solera* system, employed for blending sherry (see p. 76) is also used here for table wines. The vintage date may well indicate the age of the oldest wine in the blend. The irreverent refer to the vintage dates as 'telephone numbers'.

Madeira

Madeira is certainly the most long-lived wine in the world. Whereas a vintage port may begin to fade after thirty or forty years, and will certainly do so after sixty, a madeira can well be a hundred years old. Madeiras of the 1790s are still in existence, and the Bristol firm of Averys, and Hedges & Butler of London, still list ancient vintage madeiras. The reasons for the longevity must lie in the peculiar heating process to which madeira is subjected; this both matures and preserves the wine; and also to its fortification, not by grape brandy, but by spirit distilled from the local sugar cane.

Just as there are basically two types of sherry, so there are two types of madeira – dry and sweet. There are variations on these types, but they are made differently. The dry types are Sercial and Verdelho, which are the names of grapes; the sweet are Bual and Malmsey, also named after grapes, the Bual being Boal in Portuguese, and Malmsey being a derivative of Malvasia or Malvoisie. There are two other grape names which may be found on old madeiras – Terrantez and Bastardo, but these are now planted very sparsely.

The dry madeira types are fermented out, and undergo the heating process before much of the spirit is added, while the sweet varieties have the spirit added early to prevent fermentation and to maintain the natural sugar in the wine, exactly as with port.

The *estufagem* or heating process has traditionally been carried out by placing casks in rooms that are slowly raised to a temperature of 42 degrees centigrade, maintained at this temperature for three months, and then slowly cooled off. Now most of this is done in concrete vats in the same slow way, but at a slightly higher temperature of 50 degrees for a rather shorter period than for wines heated in cask. Only the very fine wines are now heat-treated in the old way, but this peculiar heating process is strictly government-controlled. This in itself was an adaptation of a still earlier method of leaving the casks out in the sun, as Mavrodaphne is still produced in Greece. When the madeira has been fortified it rests in wood for a year or more before being bottled. But fine madeiras will be aged for a much longer period in cask. The cheaper sweet madeiras do not have the spirit added before going through the *estufagem* process, as so much spirit is lost by evaporation in this long heating period. Such wines are treated like the Sercials and Verdelhos, and then sweetening is added afterwards.

There are three kinds of madeira: Vintage, Solera and Blended. Very little vintage madeira is now made. It went out with the two scourges of the island: the oidium or mildew disease in 1852, and the phylloxera. The trouble with vintage madeira is that it takes a great many years to mature in cask, and cannot be sold like port, two years after the vintage and immediately after bottling.

Madeira produced on the *solera* system is a blend of madeiras of various ages, some of them very old. As with sherry a proportion of the wine of different ages is drawn off and blended. An example of

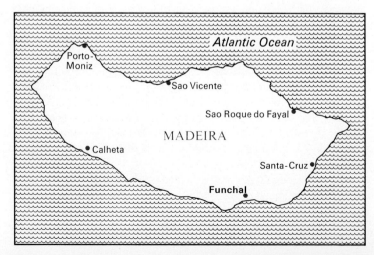

this is Blandy's Grand Cama de Lobos 1864. The *solera* from which this madeira is blended was laid down in 1864. Most fine quality madeiras are produced on the *solera* principle.

Blended madeiras are younger wines made up from different varieties and different growers' wines. They are the least expensive of madeiras. Sercial is the wine for aperitifs. It never pretends to be as dry as a Fino sherry, but it can be like a full bodied Amontillado or a dry Oloroso. Verdelho is fuller, but has a dry finish. It matures quicker than Sercial, and is more of an all-purpose wine. Bual is medium rich, and matures more speedily than the more luscious Malmsey, which is particularly full-flavoured, and has a powerful penetrating aroma. There are one or two other madeira names that may be met, among them Rainwater. This was the popular dessert wine of the American southern states in the slave-owning days. It is a blended wine, mostly Sercial.

My view is that, to be good, madeira must be reasonably old, or the product of a *solera* which includes a good proportion of old wine. As old wine is naturally more costly than young, it follows that good madeira cannot be cheap. This, of course, does not apply to madeira for more modest purposes, such as cooking, for which very large quantities are used in France, notably for *sauce madère*. The great appeal of madeira is its peculiar, slightly austere, dry finish and its unique nose. There is always a certain acidity, which holds in check the lusciousness to be found in a vintage port. Madeira has distinction of flavour which, in my view, port seldom if ever attains. It is helped by some age in bottle as well as in cask.

Madeira has been in the doldrums commercially for a long time, and trade has been adversely affected by the swing of public taste against sweet dessert wines – the 'cream' types of sherries excepted. In 1925 the Madeira Wine Association was formed by several leading British firms, who then dominated the market in much the same way as the British firms once did in Oporto. More recently other firms have joined the Association, which now consists of Blandy, Cossart Gordon, Rutherford & Miles, Leacock, and one or two other firms, including one large Portuguese house. The Association owns the stocks of all the constituent members, who draw on them for their own trade. They represent about half the trade.

The average annual production of madeira is about 600,000 gallons. Britain is only the sixth on the list of major importers – though third in terms of value – and in 1972 took about 51,000 gallons. Madeira is, in my view, the most under-rated or under-consumed of the great wines of the world, and is due for a revival in popularity.

SPAIN

Spain spells sherry to most wine-drinkers, but in fact a very wide range of table wines is made. Unfortunately, in my opinion, these have to some extent linked themselves, in Britain, with French table wine names; some have Spanish 'Chablis', 'Graves', 'Burgundy' and 'Sauternes' labels. If some vague resemblance may be found between real burgundy and the Spanish full-bodied wine, I can detect little connection with white wines, unless it be that the 'Chablis' is *fairly* dry, the 'Sauternes' *distinctly* sweet. Such names do no service either to themselves or to the wines they are named after, and will disappear under EEC stipulations.

The best table wines certainly come from the Rioja area in the north of the country. How good they can be is usually discoverable only by visiting the area itself. The red are generally better than the white in the long run, particularly those from the Alavese area. Again one need not take too seriously the ancient vintage dates on the bottles, for to some extent the solera system is used here, as with sherry. But a 'senior' Rioja is a wine of distinction, dry yet with a touch of that southern-wine flavour. A fine old Rioja has something of the dry distinction of a fine, slightly austere red Bordeaux. A wine labelled *Reserva* indicates that it is fully matured.

Nearly all Spanish wines are sold under brand names, and two large firms are Marqués de Riscal and Bilbainas, both of them Rioja firms. Other reliable firms are Murrieta and Santiago in the Rioja region, and Torres in Panadés. The finer wines from controlled areas have a seal of origin on the bottle.

Most of the inexpensive Spanish wines to be found in Britain come from Tarragona in the north-east, but on the spot they sail under the national colour of domestic brands, and not as imitations of French wines. They are full, fruity wines, not very distinguished but quaffable, particularly the reds which are on the sweet side. Tarragona is the second largest winefield, after Valdepeñas, which lies in the middle of the country. It is not a delimited area with controlled appellation, like the Rioja and several other areas. The peculiarity of these wines is that they are matured in large, Ali-Baba type pottery jars or amphorae. The wines are light, both red and white.

Good dry white wines come from Alella, north of Barcelona in Catalonia, and are normally bottled in hock-style bottles. But there are also very reasonable whites in the Panadés area, which is south of

---

opposite: Schloss Landshut at Bernkastel, on the Moselle, is one of the most romantically situated of many German vineyard castles.

the Catalan capital. From here also comes the sparkling wine Perelada, which some years ago was correctly denied, in the British law courts, the right to call itself champagne. Other sparkling wines are produced in the north of Spain, including Frexinet, Codorniu (Non Plus Ultra), Rigol and Castellblanch.

There are many other local wines which may be encountered by visitors, both on the mainland and in the Balearic Islands, but the only other significant wine outside Jerez is malaga, one of the five world-known fortified dessert wines – the others being sherry, port, madeira and marsala. It is a very deeply coloured wine, owing partly to the fact that the grapes are concentrated by heating and the spirit is added later. Like marsala it lacks the wide demand that it used to have. It is also produced as a natural, low-strength table wine, deep in colour, with a sweet muscatel flavour. As an inexpensive alternative to port as a dessert wine, it is to be recommended; one of the undeservedly unfashionable wines just now.

Much brandy is made in Spain. It is usually rather sweet and dark.

Sherry

There are essentially two types of sherry: Fino (dry) and Oloroso (basically dry but commonly sweetened). Both types are fortified by the addition of brandy, although some of the finest, driest Finos in Spain are scarcely, if at all, fortified. For the voyage abroad they are slightly dosed with brandy to hold the wine together. The fortification of sherry roughly doubles the average alcoholic strength compared with a table wine, so that it is about 20 per cent, compared with 40 per cent for the usual commercial brandy.

There are one or two special points about sherry production. First, the grapes are left in the open air after picking, so that they dry out in the hot sun. The grapes destined to produce the fuller Olorosos are left out longer to become more raisinous than those for the Finos.

The second point of interest is that in order to ensure adequate acidity for these southern wines, gypsum is added to the must. This is known as 'plastering' and was a form of 'sophistication' much denounced in Victorian times when applied to table wines. Then the fermented wine is left in the open air, and a curious phenomenon may or may not occur. A film of yeast, known as the *flor*, covers the surface of the wine in the cask. Only these *flor* sherries will become Finos. The others will develop into Olorosos. The brandy is added later, i.e. after the fermentation and not during it, as in port. A rather fuller oloroso-style dry wine developing little or no *flor* is called *Palo Cortado*, but this is rare.

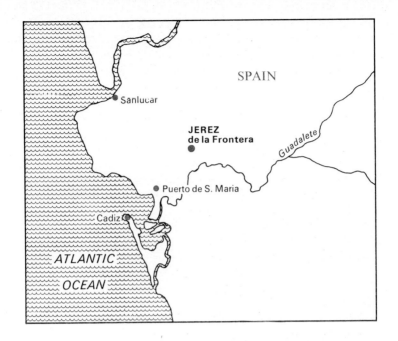

The quality of the Finos and Olorosos will of course vary according to the excellence of the original grapes and wine. Olorosos are originally dry, but their fullness arises from glycerine, formed as a by-product of fermentation; with age this develops, but the rich sherries we know are the result of added sweetness. It is, however, possible to have a very dry though full-bodied Oloroso. As marketed they will also vary according to the 'house style' of the large firms in whose hands most of the trade is concentrated. There are of course other types of sherry to be found on sherry bottle labels – Amontillado, Amoroso, Manzanilla, Cream, Brown are the best known examples, apart from the brand names of the sherry firms.

There is no vintage sherry; instead it is produced on the *solera* system. By this casks are piled up, three or four tiers high, with the young wine on the top rank, and the oldest wine in the bottom. The wine is blended downwards, so that when some is drawn off from the lowest layer of casks, it is replenished from the one above, which in turn is re-filled from the line above and so to the top. The amount taken is very carefully controlled so that the essential quality of the blend remains unaltered. It will be understood that there are a number of casks in each row. The *flor* rests on the top of the wine which is drawn out from beneath it. The stocks of casked wine of the leading Jerez firms are vast indeed, and each *solera* is backed by a chain of what might be called sub-soleras of descending age. These are known as *criaderas*, or nurseries (in the horticultural sense). The effect is of a lengthy, but intermittent, flow of sherry from the youngest to the oldest, but with the end-product a constant, standardised blend to suit the particular brand or mark.

The brandy, which is distilled from the still wine, is added before the sherry is bottled. The wine is sweetened, if required, by the addition of what is known as PX. This comes from the Pedro Ximenez grape, dried in the sun to give it the rich raisiny quality. The addition of brandy during the fermentation checks this, and leaves the wine very sweet. PX acts like the dosage in champagne. The finest Olorosos do not contain PX. There are also other cheaper wines used for sweetening.

Although all the wine for sherry is supposed to come from around Jerez there is another area which produces similar wines, near Cordoba. Its local speciality is Montilla, which, as sold abroad, is a very dry, clean wine, but in fact various types are produced there, and much used to find its way to Jerez and was used in the normal blends. The Spanish authorities have tightened up, and reduced the territorial limitations of the sherry-producing region, and so the Montilla area wines are now excluded from sherry blends. Montilla has naturally a high alcoholic strength; if bottled on the spot, it often comes in a hock-shaped bottle.

The leading sherry types are:

Fino	dry to very dry
Amontillado	rather fuller flavoured and often a little more full-bodied than Fino from which it develops with age
Amoroso	This is not one of the main styles, but indicates a full-bodied wine leaning more to the sweet side than to the dry, but not luscious
Manzanilla	A delicate, dry, sometimes slightly salty-tasting, Fino which has been matured near the sea at Sanlúcar
Oloroso	This generally suggests a sweet dessert wine, but there are dry Olorosos, although never so delicate as Finos

Italian vineyards have no 'château' or 'Schloss'. This villa on a wine estate is a typical proprietor's residence.

Cream   This indicates a very sweet, luscious dessert sherry; the original, of course, was Bristol Cream, a trade name developed from a similarly rich style first nationally associated with Bristol wine merchants. Also although all Bristol wine firms sell a Bristol Milk according to their own blend, this sherry need have no more connection with Bristol than the sweet Yugoslav white wine called Tiger's Milk has with tigers. There are now many Cream sherries, including Armada Cream and Celebration Cream. This is not surprising, for, in spite of the reported decline in the taste for sweet wines, the cream sherries lead the sherry market in Britain.

Other names on sherry bottles either have some territorial association, as for example Macharnudo Fino, which comes from a particular Jerez district noted for its Finos; or associated names such as East India, which is a dark rich sherry that, in sailing-ship days, used to be sent to the East Indies as ballast, with the object of maturing it through the ship's motion. This and Brown Sherry are generally full, sweetened types of Oloroso.

It only remains to say that there is a good deal of snobbery associated with the alleged necessity of sherry being dry – unless it is a cream sherry. As a result there are several sherries on the market which describe themselves as dry, but are nothing of the sort. It is a fact that some of the finest sherries are dry, but then other excellent wines are very sweet. There are, however, degrees of dryness, and you can take your choice from many alternative gradations; or if you like sherry a little fuller you can drink Amontillados which also vary very much in style. And so on into the richest Old Brown.

In this country sherries are either sold under the brand names of the big Jerez firms, such as Domecq, Garvey, Gonzalez Byass, La Riva, Mackenzie, Sandeman and Williams & Humbert, or they are blends made up by the requirements of wine merchants, such as Harveys, over here. Britain is the largest market in the world, with a sale of nearly 10 million gallons. There is no reason to believe that these latter house blends are in any way inferior to the advertised brands; it all depends on the skill and requirements of the wine merchants.

4 Lesser European producers

After the five great wine-producing countries of Western Europe, there are two lesser producers, Luxembourg and Switzerland, and nine others stretching from Austria to the Asian frontier in the USSR. Most of these countries are increasing the size and quality of their production, and their wines are likely to become more and more common in Britain; some, like Yugoslavian and Hungarian wines are already well established here.

WESTERN EUROPE

Luxembourg
The river Moselle on its way from France to Germany flows through Luxembourg, and on its banks white wine, similar in style to the German moselles, is produced. They are light and naturally rather acid wines, with the result that they have to be 'improved', as the Germans say, with sugar. They are fresh, with the bitter-sweet taste often to be found in sugared wines, but make agreeable drinking. Although they were imported into Britain soon after the last war, they are now scarcely available over here. An exception is one of the better sparkling wines, St Martin. Most of the wine not consumed within Luxembourg itself – the inhabitants and visitors between them annually consume a considerable quantity per head – is sold in the other Benelux countries, notably in Belgium. Anyone motoring through Luxembourg should take the opportunity of sampling the local wines, which are inexpensive. They make admirable picnic wines, embellishing the food without making one too sleepy.

The better wines have a Marque Nationale neck label, with an official number. This indicates that the wine has been approved after tasting.

Switzerland
Considering its size and mountainous character, Switzerland produces a surprising amount of wine: about 2.1 million hectolitres. It also has the not-altogether-unexpected distinction of having the highest vineyard in Europe, 4,000 feet up from sea-level at Vispertermine above the Rhône Valley. It produces wine too in 17 out of the 25 cantons.They are rather light wines, tending to have an excess of acidity. Many Swiss white wines are petillant or slightly sparkling.

There are six main wine areas: the Valais, which consists of the Rhône Valley before it enters the Lake of Geneva; the Vaud, which includes most of the vineyard area around that lake; Ticino, the Italian-speaking canton south of the St. Gothard Pass; Geneva; Neuchâtel and Zurich, mainly near the lake of that name.

The Valais wines are usually named after the grapes from which they are produced, notably the prolific Chasselas, which is there called Fendant. Another grape name on labels is Johannisberger, which is the Sylvaner grape, and Tokayer (Pinot Gris). Three rather rare but well-considered Valais white wines bear the names of local grapes: Amigne, Arvine and Humagne. They are fuller in flavour than many Swiss whites. The best known Swiss red wine, Dôle, comes from the Valais; it is a light wine and contains about 10 per cent of wine made from white grapes. A lighter type of Dôle is sold as Gorons. Another Valais wine curiosity is the white Vin du Glacier, which is made near Sion and then taken up onto the high alps to mature.

The Vaud area includes three districts: Chablais, Lavaux and La Côte. All wines of any quality are white, with district rather than grape names on the labels. The best in Chablais are Yvorne and Aigle, and in Lavaux, Dézaley and St. Saphorin. The Côte wines are lighter, centring on Morges and Begnins and on Nyon. A generic name for Vaud white wines is Dorin, for red it is Salvagnin.

The best known district in the Geneva wine area is Mandement, where light white wines are made. The Neuchâtel white wines, produced overlooking that long narrow lake, are known for their pétillance and are called 'star' wines on that account. But from this area comes one of the best and most full-bodied Swiss red wines, Cortaillod. There is a white variety too, as well as a local rosé, which is known as Oeil de Perdrix.

Sixty per cent of the Zurich canton wines are white, the rest red. The Ticinese wine has been rather looked down on, but in the last decade or so an infusion of Merlot grape from France has been introduced, and great efforts are being made to raise the standards of the red wine production. The results so far are good.

Swiss wines, red and white, are nearly all best for early drinking and do not warrant keeping. That they are as good as they are, in difficult climatic conditions, is a tribute to the skill and persistence of the Swiss viticulturists.

CENTRAL EUROPE

Austria

Basically Austria is a country of white wines, producing approximately 87% white and 13% red. The most popular red wine to be found on wine lists, Kalterersee, in fact comes from the Italian Tyrol near Bolzano, once part of the Austro-Hungarian empire. For that reason a proportion of the imports of this wine is admitted into Austria at reduced duty rates so long as it is bottled in the Austrian Tyrol. The best really Austrian red wine comes from Burgenland.

Most Austrian wine production in terms of acreage comes from the northern part of the country, known as Lower Austria, which accounts for 60% and the biggest wine area here is known as the Weinviertel (Wine Quarter), which lies north of Vienna and the Danube and extends up to the Moravian frontier in Czechoslovakia. Some very pleasant light white wines come from this region, the best of them bottled on one of the wine *Schloss* estates. Finer white wines, however – and many believe them Austria's best – come from in or near the Wachau, the delightful stretch of the Danube running between mountains, and bordered by vineyards and monasteries. These are fresh crisp wines, many made from the Grüne Veltliner grape, which may be considered Austria's leading native grape. But excellent Rieslings also come from this region, of which the main centres are Dürnstein, in whose castle Richard-Coeur-de-Lion was imprisoned, Loiben, Stein and Krems; the latter two are slightly to the east of the Wachau.

From south of Vienna, near the spa town of Baden, comes Austria's one wine with an international reputation: the white Gumpoldskirchner. Full-bodied and fresh when well made, it should be dry rather than sweet, but in the past was often 'stretched'. Now it is firmly controlled, and all authentic bottles bear a 'quality seal' issued by the Austrian Wine Institute after the wine has been tasted, and there is a control number on the bottle. To the south east and towards the Hungarian and Yugoslav frontiers lie the wine areas of Burgenland and Styria. Some red wines, such as Blaubburgunder, come from Burgenland, but many consider the white are the better. A notable sweet wine is the Ruster Ausbruch, similar to a German *trockenbeerenauslese*, deriving from near the large Neusiedlersee, also the source of grapey Muscat-Ottonel wines. Most of the Styrian wines are white, but some rosé is also produced there.

There is also a small wine area around Vienna, which consumes most of its own local produce, and a good deal more, not least in the

suburban cafés of Grinzing, Sievering and Nussdorf, which special-
ise in the *'heurige'* wine. This is the wine of the current year, or *vin
de l'année* as the French call it. By a concession dating from the days
of the Empress Maria-Theresa, the inkeepers of these places are
allowed to sell their wine tax-free, provided it comes from their own
vineyards. Since this condition has long been more honoured in the
breach than in practice, special licences now have to be obtained for
the sale of the 'heurige' wine, which, being more immature and acid
than it looks and tastes, can upset unaccustomed stomachs.

Sparkling wine is made in Austria, also Perlwein, which is semi-
sparkling or *pétillant,* i.e. the sparkle soon disappears in the glass.
The best of Austrian liqueurs is certainly the apricot brandy made in
the Wachau.

Vienna is renowned for its wine cellars, where one can buy 'open
wine' by the glass from all parts of the country.

Austrian wine production is slowly increasing, and is now about 3
million hectolitres a year. It is also improving, and the better wines
deserve more attention than they usually receive. This is partly because most are imported in bottle, to maintain their freshness, and
this puts them into competition with wines from other countries,
notably Yugoslavia and Germany.

Czechoslovakia
The wines of this country are less known abroad than those of any
other part of Central or Eastern Europe. Indeed, many people are
suprised to hear that there are any native wines at all – Bohemia in
particular being connected with beer. The reason for this is that
owing to insufficient output they are basically not exported.

There are, however, some good wines. The best are in Slovakia,
and Moravia, but there is a curiously isolated Bohemian vineyard at
Melnik on the Elbe, about twenty-five miles north of Prague, where
rather light red and white wines are made.

The centre of the wine trade is in Bratislava, capital of Slovakia,
and there are vineyards just outside the city. Slovakia produces twice
as much wine as Bohemia and Moravia combined. The best Moravian wines are from Velki Pavlovice, Maltice and Mikulov, the
last-named lying due north of Vienna near the frontier between Austria and Czechoslovakia. The red wines are light and not unlike
Beaujolais in style.

A good deal of sparkling wine is made in Czechoslovakia and it
sells under brand names, such as Château Melnik and Château
Bzenec, a Slovakian centre. Some brandy is made, but the great

southern Bohemian drink is slivovitz, made from plums. Although it is also made in other countries, the Czechs, at least, believe theirs is the best. Total wine production is around 860,000 hl.

Hungary

Hungary is regarded by its neighbours in Eastern Europe as the leading wine-producing country in that part of the world. The most famous Hungarian wine is Tokay, and both Hungarian Riesling and Bull's Blood or Egri Bikaver are known in Britain.

Wine is widely made in Hungary, from the Austrian frontier in the west to the hills of Northern Hungary, and also in the south on the Alpine foothills. The chief centres of Hungarian wine growing are around Lake Balaton, the very large fresh-water lake south-west of Budapest, with a shoreline of 180 miles. Nearly 3 million hectolitres are produced yearly.

Tokay comes from a hilly district in the north-east of the country. Its name is taken from a hill of that name, which rises to a little over 1,000 feet, but the wine-growing district includes twenty-five villages. With a soil richer than usual for wine growing, and a climate that is hot in summer and cold in winter, it is not surprising that Tokay is a distinctive wine. The chief grape is the Furmint, but some varieties of Muscatel are also employed. The same 'noble rot', which shrivels up the grapes in Sauternes and in the German wine districts, produces Tokay; the word *'aszu'*, to be found on Tokay labels, refers to these shrivelled berries. The fungus increases the sugar content by reducing the water in the grape, and it also absorbs some of the acid content. As a result a fine Tokay is a luscious wine. The *aszu* berries are kept separate from the others in special tubs known as *'puttonos'*. They are pressed separately and then used to 'fortify' the normal must which is collected in larger barrels of 30-35 gallons. The higher the proportion of *aszu* must added to the ordinary must, the richer, sweeter and fuller the wine. This is measured by the number of *puttonos*, each of which hold about 7-7½ gallons. So a Tokay labelled three *puttonos* should be richer and finer than one labelled two *puttonos*. Although six-*puttonos* Tokay is sometimes made, the top grade is normally five.

When the wine is made, it is left to mature in barrels and, unlike ordinary table wines but similar to sherry, the barrels are not topped up. The effect of this contact with the air is said to give Tokay 'a taste of bread'. Like madeira it is a very long-lived wine, and there are records of it lasting for 200 years.

Owing to the lengthy process of production and the large amount

91

of grapes needed to make Tokay *aszu,* it cannot be a cheap wine. It is all bottled on the spot in half-litre bottles, and is undoubtedly one of the great wines of the world.

Even rarer still is the almost mythical Tokay Essence. This is made from the unpressed juice of the *aszu* berries in the vats. This juice trickles out owing to the accumulated weight of the fruit. It is collected and fermented, but its sugar-content is so high that only a small proportion is transformed into alcohol, with the result that a Tokay Essence may have an alcoholic strength of only 5 per cent, and will not exceed 8 per cent, which is about the strength of a very minor German wine. It is clear that this must be an extremely expensive wine, seldom now sold, but used for blending with Tokay *aszu.*

The lesser, drier Tokay, without the *aszu* 'fortification' is called Tokay Szamarodni. Its sweetness will depend on the amount of *aszu* berries in the must. These will not have been separated from the others, but contribute their lusciousness along with the normally ripe grapes.

The chief centre of the Lake Balaton wine area is Badacsony, whence come some of the best Hungarian white dry wines. The other Lake Balaton wine widely known is Balatony Furmint, called after the grape of that name. It is a light white wine. There is also a Tokay Furmint, which merely means a wine of the Tokay area made exclusively from the Furmint grape.

Bull's Blood is certainly the best known Hungarian red wine, although it has no connection with bulls or blood, but derives its name from the deep colour of the wine, which is produced from a blend of grapes, chiefly a local one known as Kadarka, whose name originated in Albania. It is a powerful, vigorous and to me often rather coarse wine, owing to the fact that when seen over here it is usually drunk too young. It is certainly inexpensive, and can be recommended to accompany full-flavoured dishes such as steak-and-kidney pudding and, of course, goulash. Another red wine is Villány.

Those Hungarian wines which are exported in cask and bottled in the country of sale are often less good than when drunk in their place of origin. This happens with the produce from many of the other lesser wine-growing countries. They suffer from prolonged voyages under varying conditions and many are not well looked after on arrival. There is not the incentive to take great care of cheap wines, such as these, as there is with more expensive growths.

Grape harvesting using traditional equipment can still be seen in many European countries.

Yugoslavia

Wine is made in all the constituent republics, to a total of over 6 million hectolitres, and the best and most popular in Britain comes from Slovenia in the north, abutting on Austria and Hungary. In and around Lutomer and Maribor some excellent white wines are made, somewhat similar in style to the German wines, which in price they more than rival. As a result the import of these wines into Britain has enormously increased in the post-war era, and now represents about a third of the total German wine imports. Most are sold as Lutomer Rieslings and represent very good value if well looked after and carefully bottled. Otherwise they may lack freshness. Some also are bottled in Yugoslavia and marketed under brand names such as 'Senator'. The main grape in these parts is the Riesling, followed by the Sipon or Chipon, which produces a rather sweeter wine. Other popular grapes are the Traminer, Sylvaner and Sauvignon. Some of the best wine of this area comes from a village named Jerusalem, apparently so christened by weary Crusaders on their way to the

Holy Land, who settled for this area as their sworn goal. A sweet wine, known as Tiger's Milk, comes from this area, and its sales have no doubt been as much encouraged by the name as have those of Bull's Blood in Hungary. Near the Adriatic is Brda, also known for its red wine.

Further south there is a red, plummy-tasting wine made in Dalmatia called Dingac, typically Mediterranean in type, being rather sweet and alcoholic. From Serbia comes a red wine named Prokupac, which is a grape name; a wine of the same name may be found in Macedonia. The same applies to white Zilavka made both in Bosnia and Macedonia. These southern white wines are rather heavy, and often deep-coloured. Other Macedonian wines imported in this country are red Kavadarka and white Smederevka. To my mind the northern wines are consistently the best, especially when bottled on the spot.

EASTERN EUROPE

Bulgaria

Although one of the classical wine-making countries of South-East Europe, Bulgaria was hampered in its development by the five centuries of Turkish rule, which only ended with their expulsion by the Russians less than one hundred years ago. For of course the Moslem Turks were against the production of alcoholic liquors.

Modern commercial production began with the development of the co-operative movement between the two World Wars, but output was then only 2.1 million hectolitres compared with 5 million today. Since Bulgaria became a Socialist state, big developments have taken place under the state wine-producing and marketing organisation, Vinprom, formed in 1948. This controls 11 wineries and distilleries, with many branches and cellars throughout the country; for wine is made all over Bulgaria, from the Black Sea coast in the east and the Danube valley in the north, to the Maritza valley in the south. No less than 70% of annual output is exported, with the Soviet Union as the largest buyer, but with Western Germany a major purchaser in the West. At present Bulgaria stands 11th in total output among the wine-producing countries, but in the next decade or so it is planned to treble output. The Bulgarians are regular wine drinkers too, with a per capita consumption of 29 bottles a year.

Broadly speaking, the wines are named after grapes, and 60% is red wine. The red wine grapes are Gamza – the most popular wine, named after a local grape and made in several areas – Mavroud, Pamid and Kadarka. Trakia (Thrace) is a light 'claret-style' red wine made from the Mavroud and Pamid grapes in the proportion of 60 to 40. It comes mostly from the south. The leading native white wine grapes are the Dimiat and Misket, and the former is the chief constitutent of Bulgarian brandy, sold under the names of Preslav, the best, and Pliska.

Gamza varies slightly according to where it is made, but is basically a fairly full wine of what we might call burgundy-style. Mavroud is full-flavoured too and probably the best Bulgarian red from a native grape. Pamid is light, almost a rosé. Dimiat, sometimes found in the country under its export name of Klosterkeller, is the commonest Bulgarian white; it is drier than the more full-bodied Misket. Sweeter wines include Hemus, also made from the Misket grape, Turnovo, a fortified dessert wine, and Tamianka, a Muscat-tasting wine.

In addition to these native grape wines, the Bulgarians have skilfully introduced a number of grape varieties from the West, including Cabernet and Chardonnay from France and Sylvaner from Germany. In my view the Cabernet is the best Bulgarian red wine, with a distinct claret flavour. The white Chardonnay also has something of the style of its native Burgundy, and is fresh and crisp, whereas most Bulgarian wines are on the full, even heavy side. These wines, and the Sylvaner are imported into Britain and retail at about 65p-75p. The native wines may also be found here, but to taste a full range of Bulgarian wines one must go to the country.

Cyprus

Cyprus has a very ancient and honourable tradition of wine-making, dating from classical times. Later its reputation and its exports received a filip, when the Crusaders established themselves on the island. Among the earlier mediaeval admirers of Cyprus wine is said to have been Richard Coeur de Lion. In the famous 'Feast of the Five Kings' held in the Hall of the Vintners' Company in London in 1362 and suitably commemorated there today in an inscription, the famous Commandaria wine was served, doubtless as a compliment to the Cypriot King, Peter I, who was present with his fellow monarchs of England, Scotland, France and Denmark.

Commandaria is certainly *the* famous wine of Cyprus, in the same way as marsala is of Sicily. It was so-called from the Grand Commandery of the Knights Templar who had their headquarters in a castle near Limassol, which to-day is the centre of the Cyprus wine trade. It is a rich dessert wine, whose grapes have been dried out before pressing, to produce a concentrated raisin-like flavour. It starts off by being a sweet red wine, but with age it becomes tawny in tinge. Like all other Cyprus wines it suffered a decline in the eighteenth and nineteenth centuries, but in recent years a determined effort, backed by the British Government, has been made to raise the standard of Cypriot viticulture and wine-making. Commandaria is certainly a wine to be considered for those who like an inexpensive sweet dessert wine to drink with fruits and nuts.

Cyprus has gained hitherto from being part of the British Commonwealth in that there has been a duty preference and the wines have been of a higher strength than foreign wines without attracting higher duties. So in recent years Cyprus wines have been cheaper than some rivals. This applied above all to the Cyprus sherry-type wines. Among the well-known brands are Emva, Monte Cristo and Mosaic, of which Emva is the most popular. No one would pretend that they equal the quality of a fine Spanish Oloroso, but they are a great deal less in price and cheaper even than the richer South African sherries. In 1972 the import of Cyprus wine into Britain was nearly 5 million gallons out of an export total of 6 million gallons; whereas in 1960 Britain had imported only 750,000 gallons of Cyprus wine.Otherwise much of it used to go for blending in the Common Market countries, whose tariff wall now limits the prospects of wine-exporting countries like Cyprus, and may affect her trade with Britain. Cyprus also produces and exports brandy, and one of the significant customers for this is the USSR.

Greece
When people think of Greek wine they usually consider only its famous resinated wine, Retsina. This is usually, but not always, a white wine but there is a red or rosé variety called Kokkinelli. Most of it comes from Attica, and it is produced from rather light, undistinguished wines. Although Retsina is alleged to be an acquired taste, there is no moral obligation on the wine drinker to acquire it! Certainly I find the penetrating flavour of the resin unattractive, but the rather less powerful Kokkinelli is more acceptable to me than the white. All these wines have to be drunk young, so if bought in Britain the question to ask the merchant is not how old it is but how young.

Fortunately there are other more easily quaffable Greek wines, some of them standardised wines sold under brand names, such as Hymettus, produced by the Athens firm of Cambas, and Demestica from Clauss in Patras. Both red and white wines bear these labels. Greek table wines are usually relatively high in alcoholic strength, like most Mediterranean wines.

Probably the most famous Greek wine is the Peloponnesian Mavrodaphne, popular partly perhaps on account of its attractive name. It is a high-strength wine, rather like a sweet sherry or madeira, and the barrels are left out in the sun to mature for four to six years. It is really too powerful to drink with food, although the Greeks do so without obvious ill-effects.

From the islands there is a relatively dry Samos, and there is a sweet Samos Muscatel, which is very luscious indeed, without, of course, the quality of the greater sweet white wines of the world. The Cretan wines are honest, clean wines, again mostly sold under brand names. The rosés are attractive and dry. Wines are made on Rhodes and other islands.

Not the least virtue of Greek wines consumed on the spot is that they are very cheap – around 30p a bottle, or even less. However, by the time they arrive here the freight and duty inevitably put them in the 60p-70p class.

The famous Greek aperitif is Ouzo, which is aniseed-flavoured and distinctly powerful. Like its French branded equivalent, Pernod, it is calculated to deaden rather than encourage the appetite. Total Greek wine production is about 4.7 million hectolitres.

Romania
Romanian wine-production is of great antiquity, dating from many centuries B.C. and, less under the control of the Turks than Bulgaria, has had a more continuous tradition. Today the Romanian Peoples' Republic regards its vineyards as an important part of the national economy, and a valuable export product. Thus great efforts have been made in the last fifteen years to increase both quality and quantity of production. A total vineyard area of 300,000 hectares has now been extended to 345,000 hectares and will be 400,000 by 1975. It will, of course, take longer before the young vineyards are in full production. Output today is nearly 8 million hectolitres.

Production is dominated by the state farms all over the country, and they provide much of the export trade, run by Fructexport of Bucharest. But the widespread co-operatives also grow grapes for wine, and this is made by one or other of the many wineries of Vinalcool, which also exports wine and spirits. While the biggest market lies in the socialist countries, particularly the Soviet Union, a very substantial trade is done with West Germany. The main research station with extension vineyards and several branches is at Valea Calugareasca about 40 miles north of Bucharest. Here new varieties are always being tried out, including grapes from Western Europe.

Some of these varieties associated with the West are widely grown in Romania, whose vineyards are scattered on the foothills of the Carpathians in Wallachia and Moldavia, on the wide plains of the latter, in Transylvania in the Tirnave area, and in the south-west near the Danube. The best red wine in my opinion is the Cabernet, of which there are several types, depending on their origin. Dealul Mare and Cotesti are usually considered the best. The latter at least is available in Britain. Although such western grapes as the Merlot and Pinot Noir are also grown, sparsely as yet, the other red wines are mostly from native grapes, the Babeasca Negra, which produces a full, slightly sweet wine and the Kadarka, another rather full-bodied sweetish wine from a grape commonly grown in Balkan wine countries, The Romanians, like wine-drinkers in other Central and Eastern European countries, enjoy big red wines with a touch of sweetness.

They have a similar taste for white wines, so that they are full-flavoured and not the crisp dry wines popular in Western Europe. Their best dry white wines probably come from Tirnave, where the Italian Riesling is widely cultivated, but it has some of the slight sweetness we find in many of the medium-quality German Rhine wines. The local white wine grapes are the Feteasca Alba and Feteasca Regale, which produce a full-bodied white wine. Other white wine grapes to be found include the Pinot Gris, the Furmint, associated more with Hungary, and the Sauvignon and Aligoté of France. Particularly appreciated are the sweet dessert wines, notably Murfatlar from near the Black Sea, Cotnari from northern Moldavia and Muscat Ottonel, grown in most wine areas. The first two are probably Romania's most distinctive wines.

A good deal of sparkling wine is produced in several areas, all made by the champagne method of secondary fermentation in bottle, and there universally called champagne: it tends to be sweet, for that is how they like it. So is the brandy (always known as 'Koniac'), with those additions of vanilla and caramel to be found in Balkan brandies, but by no means undrinkable. The best variety is Milkov; a common brand is Dacia. The popular aperitif is the plum brandy Tuica (pronounced 'sweeca') which can vary considerably in strength. A local vermouth is Carpathi, sweetish in style. In Britain the prices of Romanian wines are modest, around 65p-70p a bottle.

But as with other wine-producing countries outside the EEC, discriminatory tariffs may make such wines more expensive and/or more difficult to obtain here.

USSR

A great deal of wine is made in the southern regions of the Union, and much more is planned. Currently total production is in the region of about 19 million hectolitres. As in other Eastern European countries grape-growing, some of it for table grapes and raisins, is taken very seriously. This is as it should be for the vine almost certainly had its birth in this part of the world, perhaps in Trans-Caucasia, perhaps further south or east. In pre-Revolutionary times the wines esteemed by the rich were those imported from the west, particularly champagne . The Russian nobility, headed by the Grand Dukes, were famed or notorious for their taste for extremely sweet champagne. Whereas a really dry champagne at the dosage may receive a half, or one per cent of sugar, the champagne exported to Russia before 1917 were dosed to the extent of 7, 8, or even, I have been told in Rheims, 12 per cent of pure cane sugar diluted in brandy. No such champagne is produced these days.

Nevertheless, there is no doubt that the Russians do like sweet wines, and Soviet sparkling wine, called 'champagne' in its own country, but bearing such names as Krasnodar when exported, is certainly on the sweet side, though not to çi-devant grand ducal standards. It is often however, but not exclusively, made by the champagne method, and it is by no means bad. A Russian rosé sparkling wine is obtainable in Britain.

This sweet taste persists in dessert wines, and fortified wines of port- and madeira-style. The Russians are particularly proud of the madeira-type wines made in the Crimea.

Although little exported, the Bessarabian red and white wines are said to be among the best table wines. Originally planted with grapes from the West, some at least have familiar grape names, such as Riesling, Fetyeska and Kabernet. They tend to be dry.

The Southern Crimea is chiefly noted for dessert wines: sherry, port and madeira types, as well as muscat wines. A centre of production is the Massandra wineries in the Yalta region. There are pink as well as white muscat wines; one of the latter is called Levadia. A Massandra sweet muscatel is imported into this country. The Riesling grape is grown here, producing a much sweeter, fuller wine than is associated with it in the West. A Tokay-type wine is also made around Massandra.

It is the Georgian wines which are most commonly found in Britain, notably Mukuzani No. 4 and Saperavi No. 5 red, and Tsinandali No. 1 and Gurdjurni No. 3 white. I have sampled these wines in Britain, and on the whole I have found them disappointing, owing to their bad condition, i.e. oxydised. However, I have tasted one or two Soviet table wines bottled on the spot, and these have been distinctly superior. I can only assume, therefore, that often they have not been well handled somewhere *en route* from the wineries to our own tables. Where the blame lies I do not know, but in view of the keenness of the Soviet oenologists to raise their quality, and the trading organisations' desire to increase their exports, it is reasonable to expect that standards will rise.

Armenia is best known for its brandy, which on a three-star level I can testify to being excellent – although I wish they would not darken it so much; and there is sometimes a strong whiff of vanilla. But Armenian brandy is a great deal better than many so-called imitations of cognac elsewhere in the world.

5 Other continents

Other continents

This chapter is necessarily brief, for this book is principally concerned with wine countries whose produce may be found in Britain. This excludes a number of wine-producing countries, principally in South America, although Chile, perhaps the best of them, does export an excellent red Cabernet wine. So far as Britain is concerned, the USA is a marginal wine country only, but it is important enough to be included, and its better wines may be found here.

Australia

Australian wine growing has a history almost as old as the early colonisation of the country. The first vineyards were planted in the Sydney region, and the first recognition of Australian wine was in 1822, when the Royal Society of Arts in London awarded a silver medal to Gregory Blaxland for his red wine. Each state or wine area has its pioneers, English, German and French, but the father of the finer Australian wines was certainly James Busby, a Northumbrian, born in Edinburgh in 1801. He arrived in Australia in 1824, and with viticulture as a hobby he planted vines on land granted to him in the Hunter River Valley. Although he was less than ten years in Australia, he began a tradition of fine wine-making that has never died out, although it has been very badly hit at various periods, particularly in the slump conditions of the inter-war years. Today a growing band of Australian wine connoisseurs look on the Hunter River area much as English wine amateurs regard the slopes of the Côte d'Or in Burgundy or the level vineyards of the Médoc. In Australia these wines are usually colloquially called clarets, although the grape most used is the Shiraz or Hermitage, varieties usually associated with the Rhône. However, some of these wines have a distinct Bordeaux taste, more perhaps like St Emilions than Médocs. This area only produces half of one per cent of Australian wine production.

South Australia is much the largest wine-producing state, responsible for about 67 per cent. New South Wales accounts for 20, Victoria about 10 per cent, Western Australia produces about 5 per cent, while in Queensland there is a little marginal wine-making only around Roma. Total Australian output is about 2.9 million hectolitres annually, of which less than 5 per cent is exported.

The heart of the South Australian wine area is the Barossa Valley, which was largely colonised by German immigrants. It is not al-

Australian vineyards are noted for their rich soil and abundant fertility **(above)**. The Dutch Baroque style of the farmhouse **(below)** is typical of many South African vineyards.

together surprising, therefore, that one of the best wines from the valley is a white Barossa Riesling,which is imported into Britain and sells at about 75p. Of the many Rieslings imported from countries other than Germany and France (Alsace) the Barossa wine stands high, and when well bottled is fresh and attractive.

Rather more than half the annual Australian grape production goes for brandy and wine spirit, used for fortifying wines. Australian brandy is by no means bad, and the best is distilled in pot-stills. It does tend to be unnecessarily dark in colour, owing to added colouring matter, and is sometimes over-sweetened with vanilla.

The rest of Australian wine production is concentrated on fortified wines, which account for about 60 per cent of wine, as opposed to spirit, production. Most of the fortified wines are of the sweet variety, and fairly strong alcoholically, but there is now available a *flor fino* sherry style wine from the Barossa, which is excellent in its class. It is sold in Britain at about the same price as South African sherry, and is in quality a serious rival for those who like inexpensive dry sherries.

Table wine production is increasing, and so is wine drinking. The *per capita* consumption in Australia is annually about 12 bottles – considerably higher than in the United Kingdom. Most of the vineyard expansion has come from the 'irrigated' areas of Victoria, New South Wales and South Australia. This irrigation is necessary owing to the heat and lack of rain, but the result is large fleshy grapes that produce wine without much distinction of flavour. The non-irrigated areas include parts of South Australia, among them the Barossa Valley, the Western Australian Swan Valley, where that state's wine production is concentrated, and the Hunter River Valley.

Some excellent sparkling wine is made, the best of it by the champagne method. Perhaps the best known is Great Western, named after its place of origin in Victoria. In Britain these wines are, very properly, not sold as champagne, although that is their general name in Australia.

So far as Australian wine in Britain is concerned, the traditional pattern was set a generation or two ago, when English maiden ladies, who would have thought it almost a little 'fast' to be detected drinking a bottle of French wine, gratefully drank 'health-giving' Australian 'burgundy' from flagons, which to the uninitiated did not look like wine bottles at all. But this has not helped the reputation of Australian wine.

Although some Australian wine is still sold in flagons, the pattern of imports into Britain is changing and developing. Partly owing to heavy freight costs and a Commonwealth duty preference, benefiting most the cheaper wines, it has remained at the inexpensive end of the wine list. The finer Australian table wines, shipped in bottle, cannot sell for much less than £1 a bottle, and at that price are uncompetitive with European wines. The result is that the wines we see in Britain are for the most part wholesome, standardised, and not very distinguished, and uncompetitive in price with the lesser European wines. Entry into the EEC, and the consequent loss of duty preference will make Australian wines dearer.

There are, however, some excellent Australian table wines, and the Australian Wine Centre, 25 Frith Street, Soho, London W1, representing a very efficiently-run industry, has a large range. As with all hot-country wines, Australian wines often lack acidity, and have a flavour which a distinguished European wine amateur has unkindly characterised as 'kangeroo'. This is partly owing to the ferruginous character which was so acceptable to the maiden ladies already mentioned, but not all Australian wines are like this, as I hope I have shown. That Australian wine can be very good was demonstrated not so long ago when a small parcel of thirty-year-old Malbec (named after the grape) from Victoria was discovered in the cellars of a wine concern moving from its old premises in London. With a remarkable fine aroma, it tasted like a distinguished but not too sweet red burgundy.

South Africa

Wine-growing is of respectable antiquity in South Africa, and the trade celebrated its tercentenary in 1955, for 1655 was the date when wines were first planted by Van Riebeck, the Governor of what later became the Cape Province. Wine was first made in 1659, but it was France which unwittingly encouraged the rivalry in wine-production, as in other fields, by the Revocation of the Edict of Nantes in 1685. A few years later displaced French Huguenots began to settle in the Cape, and some turned their attention to wine-making. In time the Cape produced the one non-European wine which has ever achieved parity of esteem with the great wines of France and Germany – Constantia, named after a forty-acre estate, called Groot Constantia, planted in 1679. This was a luscious dessert wine, both red and white. The formula, if that be the right word, of its production was lost in the decline that overcame the Cape vineyards from about 1830 onwards. But it so happens that a few years ago I was given the opportunity of tasting a Constantia of the 1830s. It was bottled in pint bottles and in style it resembled a fine old madeira, with a splendid aroma and plenty of flavour and body.

The decline in Cape wine production arose both from over-production and the gradual ending of discrimination against French wines in the nineteenth century. Only in 1918 did the industry begin to pick up, with the formation of a farmers' co-operative, called the Ko-Operative Wijnbouwers Vereniging, and commonly known as KWV. The original total of 1940 wine famers who joined it has now increased to nearly 5,000. The KWV was progressively given semi-official control over the South African wine trade. It controls all spirit distillation and fixes minimum wine prices. Independent producers must sell wine through or with the consent of KWV, which sells 90 per cent of all South African wine exported. To prevent over-production, quotas are fixed for wine farmers, many of whom also grow fruit. The South African wine industry is probably more strictly controlled than any other in the world. If the KWV seems autocratic, it is also successful. There are at least eight important firms which do not belong to the KWV, including:

Twee Jongezellen Estate	Monis Wineries
Nederburg Estate	Alphen Estate
Bellingham Estate	Bertrams
Stellenbosch Farmers Wineries	Stellenvale

As in the early days production is still almost entirely confined to the extreme south-west corner of Cape Province. There are three districts: the Coastal Belt, which includes Stellenbosch, Constantia, and Paarl, the centre of the wine industry about forty miles from Cape Town, the Little Karoo, centring on Worcester, Robertson and Montagu; and a small intermediate area around Ceres and Caledon.

As in Australia, the question of irrigation is important, and as there the best table wines are made in the non-irrigated areas. The best light red wines are made at Constantia and Stellenbosch, and broadly speaking they grow heavier as they go inland. In the Little Karoo the vineyards are irrigated and dessert wines are made. More white than red table wines are made, partly no doubt owing to the demand for wines that can be served fresh and cool in a hot climate. These table wines are standardised similarly to those common in Australia. They are sound rather than exciting. The white wines are drunk very young, and the red wines will be at their best from about five to ten years old. In such an equable climate there are few variations in vintage. Among the best wines that I have tasted in Britain are the Nederburg red and white, estate bottled. The white Nederburg Riesling, fresh but with considerable flavour, is certainly one of the better wines made from German grapes outside Europe. It is generally accepted that the red wines are better than the white.

There has been an upsurge of wine drinking in South Africa in the last decade or so. The sale of table wines inside South Africa rose from 22.5 million gallons in 1965 to 35.2 million gallons in 1970, while the sales of fortified wines in the latter year were 11.7 million gallons. Wine production in South Africa has now reached about $3\frac{3}{4}$ million hectolitres a year. Of this about 50 per cent is used for distillation and the rest for various types of wine. In Britain the picture of South African wines is quite a different one for it is dominated by South African sherry, which at home is not a particularly popular drink. South African wine imports only picked up after their decline when preferential rates of duty were given in 1925 to Empire wines, as they were then called. The fortified wine duty is lower per bottle than the current foreign rate, and until British entry into the EEC this gave a great boost to the South African sherry industry. Combined with this, it was discovered that the famous *flor,* which bred on young sherry and gave the peculiar character to dry sherries, was not only native to Spain, but was also to be found on grapes grown in South Africa. The sales of South African sherry, while substantial, are rather less than a few years ago. In 1971 about 1.5 million gallons were sold in Britain, compared with nearly 10 million gallons of Spanish sherry.

The South Africans deserve praise for having agreed with the French Government not to use French wine names such as 'Sauternes' or 'Burgundy'. This, of course, does not apply to sherry. Moreover it does not bind their customers in Britain, where one sees French names affixed to South African wines bearing the names of blends thought up by their marketers in Britain. One cannot altogether blame the latter, for the main European wine regions have placed such a stamp of their personality on wines all over the world that it is easy and comprehensible for all of us to use these standards as a measure of comparison. Nevertheless one must applaud those countries which stand on their own.

North African Countries
All the countries on the southern shores of the Mediterranean produce wine, and most of them are now trying to develop and market their production. Algeria, thanks to the French and to suitable climate and soil, certainly leads the field both in quality and quantity.

The quantity, formerly about 10 million hl., is now much reduced and little of it goes to France.

The best Algerian wines come from the slopes of the Atlas mountains and thus are not over-exposed to torrid heat. Algerian wines are full-bodied and if kept for a sufficient period can turn out surprisingly well, as those will remember who put aside a little of the Algerian wine imported in bulk in the latter half of the last war. Algerian 'claret' with four or five years bottle age is no despicable drink.

Some sound red wine is made in Morocco, and is imported into Britain to sell at around 60p-65p – one of the cheapest red wines that can be bought here. It is soft and usually rather lacking in acidity. Much the same applies to Tunisian wines, which are made in two co-operatives on the outskirts of Tunis. The white wines that I have tasted have had little flavour, the rosés were better, and some of the red on much the same level as the Moroccan. Both countries send most of their wine to France or to former French possessions in Africa. Some also goes to Germany for blending. Tunis annually produces about $\frac{1}{2}$ million hectolitres, Morocco over 1 million hectolitres.

United States of America

Wine growing in the USA has a surprisingly long history, for the first Californian vineyard was planted in the eighteenth century by the missionary priests; the oldest California winery dates from 1775. For many years the commercial centres of wine production were in the East, in New York State and New Jersey, and in Ohio. Wine is still produced in these states; indeed no fewer than twenty-nine states claim to be wine-producers, but the emphasis has now shifted decisively to California, which accounts for 75 per cent of the sale of wine, including imported wine, in the country. As imported wine accounted for over 10 per cent of sales, California wines were responsible for over 80 per cent of the sales of American wines, whose total output in 1971 was about 8 million hectolitres.

Outside California wines are largely made from the hybrid vines which are prohibited in France, and indeed in California. A good deal of sparkling wine is made in New York State, and an equal amount in California. Little of this is made by the *méthode champenoise;* most is made by the tank method. Nevertheless it is called champagne, much to the irritation of the French producers of authentic champagne.

Indeed, the Americans have seized on European 'generic' names even more than other wine countries, so that 'chablis', 'burgundy' and 'sauterne' (without the final 's' of the original) are common, although not closely resembling the wines from which their names are derived. This difference in style applies even more to California 'sherry', although some dry *flor* sherry is now being produced.

The other, broadly more informative, and reliable way of naming American wines is from the grape, such as Pinot Chardonnay, Riesling-Sylvaner or Cabernet. This is the practice of the better wine producers of California, where an enthusiastic and growing knowledgeable army of wine drinkers is helping to create a demand for something better than the 'standard' wines which characterise American wine production.

There are three main producing areas in California: in the north near San Francisco; in the inland valleys around Sacramento and Fresno; and in the southern region in the neighbourhood of Los Angeles. The hot inland and southern areas are most suitable for dessert wines, and the best table wine area is in the northern valleys, notably Napa, Livermore, Sonoma and Santa Clara. Their altitude and proximity to the Pacific produces a more suitable climate for fine wine production. The Napa Valley is generally considered the best area and there are some well-known vineyards and proprietors. One of these is Beaulieu, owned by Georges de Latour. His wines are available in Britain, through Avery of Bristol, and I have been able to taste some of them. A four-year-old white Pinot Chardonnay was a dry wine of distinction, and so was a thirteen-year-old red Cabernet Sauvignon, distinctly St Emilion-like in character. Other Californian producers of particularly good wines include the Christian Brothers (whose wines are available in the UK), Concannon, Heitz, Charles Krug, Martini and Martin Ray. Korbel is a fine sparkling wine made by the champagne method, and called champagne by the producers. Other British importers of American wines are Stowells and Saccone & Speed, but on a small scale. For although California wine has been sold in Britain since the last century, its high production costs and freight charges make it uncompetitive here with European wines.

In America itself, however, domestic wines are inexpensive. Americans are now drinking more wine per head of population than we are in Britain: twelve bottles annually compared with seven bottles. Although it is Scotch whisky imports that are highlighted, wine imports from the Continent are rising fast. At one time most of these were Italian, owing to the great number of Italian immigrants in the country, but increasingly it is the finer wines of France and Germany which are being sought.

6 Drinks before meals

Aperitifs

The word is French, and France is the home of aperitifs. The basic idea is to stimulate the gastric juices and at the same time to produce a suitably relaxed atmosphere for one's guests and oneself before sitting down to a meal. Contrary to common belief, alcohol is in fact a sedative and not a stimulant, and before a meal one does not need too much of it – especially if there is wine at the meal; strong liquor in quantity deadens the palate. Consequently on occasions when fine wine is served, I think that fortified, sparkling or even dry still wines are often more appropriate than spirits or cocktails. So far as acting as appetisers and stimulants of the gastric juices are concerned, it is generally recognised that dry rather than sweet drinks are more effective, for the latter tend, like sweets before meals, to take the edge off the appetite. If slimming is your aim, that is another matter.

Some French aperitifs, like Pernod, are so powerful and so strongly flavoured – with aniseed in this case – that after a couple you may feel either on the top of the world or somewhere in its depths. Your palate will also have had a pretty powerful blow – with the meal, the wine and the company yet to be faced. So some of the lighter aperitifs are preferable, leaving spirits and the powerful branded aperitifs for the coming-home pick-me-up an hour or two before dinner. Obvious choices among the brands are Dubonnet and the Italian Campari, Carpano, Gancia Americano and Punt è Mes. However, there is a great deal to be said for Vermouths, either plain or with a twist of lemon in them. For this purpose I prefer the drier varieties, such as Noilly Prat, but there is nothing 'right' or 'wrong' about it, and if you find these too dry and prefer the sweeter Italian Vermouths, particularly in warm weather, there are several million other Vermouth drinkers in accord. I rather favour Carpano, which, as is the way in republican Italy, has been called 'the king of vermouths', and Punt è Mes ('a point and a half'), a distinctive astringent aperitif said to have been christened by stockbrokers to accustomed to dealing in 'points'. But my favourite Vermouth is Chambéry; it is very herby, slightly sweeter than the fashionable French Vermouths, but drier than the Italian. Few of the French outside the region of Savoy, where it is made, have heard of it.

However, for the all-purpose aperitif there is certainly no better drink than sherry, for there are so many gradations of style and flavour, from the dryest of bone dry sherries such as Tres Palmas, San Patricio and Tio Pepe, to the richest Olorosos, such as the various Bristol Milks, Bristol Cream, Old Browns and Armada Cream.

In this chapter we are talking about aperitif sherries, so we concentrate on the dry to medium dry. Sherry is a white wine, and like all dry white wines, the dry varieties should be served cool and fresh. Drunk like this it tastes much crisper and more lively. Warm pub sherry is even worse than warm pub beer. In summer I use a refrigerator – about 40 minutes – but in winter outside the back door or on a window sill is good enough. Sherry should not be excessively chilled, for that destroys both aroma and flavour. I find that in winter I like a rather fuller type of sherry than in summer, even an Amoroso on a cold evening, and this should not be chilled. In summer I find a Fino or a Manzanilla attractively fresh. In winter really dry, but full-flavoured Amontillados and Olorosos are very acceptable. Not all sherries labelled dry are so, owing to the odd snobbism that one should prefer sherry dry. One well-known brand is in fact sweetened Oloroso.

Dry Port
There are those who say this is a contradiction in terms, for port is taken to be a fruity, full-blooded wine, and traditionalists' faces go almost a vintage red at the idea of White Port. But a dry tawny port – which means one aged in wood – can make an excellent aperitif; although it should be a dry wine, sold sometimes under such a name as Dry Aperitif Port. White Port is something different. It is made from white grapes, and matures more quickly than wine from red grapes. It can be quite as dry as some sherries sold as such, and with the fullness of flavour one associates with port. Such a wine should be chilled like dry sherry.

Madeira
An excellent alternative to sherry before a meal is a dry madeira, either a Sercial or a Verdelho. Just as a rather fuller sherry may be specially agreeable in winter, so a dry madeira, which, owing to its method of production, has a certain built-in dryness that is lacking in dry ports, makes a most acceptable winter aperitif, whether or not wine is to follow. My own preference is a Sercial, and it may be served at room temperature, although in summer it can be a little fresher to the taste if slightly chilled.

Some examples of the different bottle shapes

Left to right: **Back row**   Moselle, hock, vintage port, white
table wine, claret
     Middle row   Champagne, burgundy, Portugese
table wine, white Bordeaux, sherry
     Back row   Chianti flask, Scotch whisky, white
rum, cognac, Italian sparkling wine

Cocktails

This is not the place for cocktail recipes, but one or two mixed drinks may be mentioned. The lighter styles of rum, such as Bacardi, are particularly suitable for these. The most famous rum thirst quencher is Cuba Libré, which is a light rum, mixed with a Cola drink and ice. The other popular rum drunk is the Daiquiri. The standard recipe is 2 ounces each of Bacardi, or other light rum, and of the juice of a lime – or equivalent of lemon juice, although of course this is not quite the same thing – and a teaspoonful of sugar with ice. It tastes even better if served in a large chilled glass. Grenadine is sometimes substituted for the sugar. Limes have a particular affinity with rum, especially the lighter types.

A refreshing summer aperitif is Campari with Perrier water or soda, served slightly chilled. Gin, and particularly vodka, are chosen for cocktails owing to their lack of penetrating flavour, but before a wine meal it is unwise to overdo the spirit content in any cocktail, as it certainly anaesthetises one against tasting the more delicate and less alcoholic beverage wines.

Aperitif Wines

There is a good deal to be said, particularly but not exclusively in summer, for serving a dry white wine as an aperitif. There are several advantages. It is less alcoholic than a fortified wine, and this is a help when there is to be wine at the following meal, for some people are a little nervous of having to drink too much. It serves as a very good introduction to other wines. Indeed I have often found it a good idea to serve a round as an aperitif and finish the bottle or bottles at table, whether or not there is some other wine to follow. Another advantage is that white wine can be an inexpensive form of aperitif. One wants to choose wines, such as Yugoslav Riesling, Alsace Sylvaner, one of those cheap Alsace wines with brand names, or a light moselle, such as a Wiltinger Riesling from the Saar tributary. A light rosé of the dryer sort is not out of place on such an occasion. Needless to say these wines should all be served fresh but not frozen.

The best of all aperitif wines is, without doubt, champagne; and it need not be madly expensive, as a bottle will just do for eight people. A non-vintage wine is quite good enough for such occasions and most wine merchants have their own 'house' champagne which can be excellent, although the poor varieties may also be sharp and green – a sample half bottle will tell you.

But there are reasonable alternatives, such as sparkling moselle and hock – known as *Sekt* in Germany, for the word champagne is banned there for German sparkling wine. It is usually a shade sweeter and grapier than a really dry champagne and lacks its firm crispness. It is also cheaper. Better is the attractive,not-too-expensive sparkling Saumur, made compulsorily by the champagne method on the Loire. Nor is sparkling white burgundy to be looked down on. It can be as crisp and fresh as many champagnes, and again, noticeably cheaper. Sparkling Vouvray tends to be rather sweeter, but there are dry Astis, the Italian sparkling wines, for those who like them.

This book is not concerned with food, but I suggest that all aperitifs should be accompanied by something to eat, whether dry biscuits, potato crips or olives, preferably the green variety; nothing too spicy. Normally one's stomach is empty when the glass of sherry or champagne comes round, and the effect is considerable lessened if there is some tit-bit to go with it. The more powerful the drink the greater the need for food; which is why the Greek (absinthe-style) Ouzo is always accompanied by a small dish of *metzes*.

7 Wines with meals

The bulk of wines go best with food; the wine tastes better and so does the food, and to my mind of the two the food is the chief gainer. For although a bottle of, say, beaujolais, does not go down well on its own, and the food tastes much the same with or without wine, yet an enjoyable bottle of wine can transform even a sandwich or bread-and-cheese meal.

We in Britain are exceptionally fortunate in the matter of wine. In France it is rare indeed to find an Italian wine, and vice versa, and it is not easy in Germany to buy a good bottle of sherry, for in all the wine-growing countries you normally expect to rely on the local produce. But here we have wine flowing in from almost every wine growing country in the world, from Chile to the Soviet Union, and Australia to Morocco; we have an unrivalled choice. But variety brings its own problems, and certainly the choice is confusing. Quite apart from the problems of price and vintage, any wine merchant will have a wide assortment of white and red table wines. There may be three or four whites from several parts of France, from Spain, Portugal, Greece, Yugoslavia, South Africa, Italy, Germany, Austria, Switzerland, Hungary and elsewhere. The variety of red wines will be no less, with many more sub-divisions of name and style from the red wine areas.

What goes with which food? Here I confess not to share a common view that it does not matter. It is suggested that if you like to drink vintage port with roast goose there is every reason why you should do so. Now there is no justifiable *moral* or *social* or *etiquette* reason why you should not do so. It is not like the alleged 'crime' of performing the difficult task of eating peas on your knife. Nor is it 'immoral' to drink white wine warm and red straight out of the refrigerator; but it does not mean that this is the way to get the best out of the wine, or to enjoy it most. With the enormous variety of wines to be drunk with food, it is scarcely surprising that some respond best one way and some another, or that certain food goes better with some types of wine and some with others. However, it is far less complicated than many people think. There is not an excessive amount of 'home work' to be done on wine, but certain things are worth knowing.

First, let us clear the ground of certain wine myths. There is no basis for the often-heard remark 'red wine with red meat – white wine with white meat'. Both go equally well with either and there is not the slightest reason why they should not do so. Nor is there any truth in the suggestion that one should drink burgundy with game, and claret or other light, dry red wines with butchers' meat. It is immaterial, and according to personal choice or what you happen to have in the home.

There *is* a fair warning over fish, and strongly flavoured dishes. Wine is on the whole rather delicate in flavour; even quite rough young red wines will not taste much if put up against curry or horseradish sauce. And if you are drinking red wine or a dry white wine, it will receive rather a jolt if you take a mouthful immediately after apple sauce or red currant jelly. Similarly, most fish makes the more delicate red wines taste slightly metallic, while white wines are not affected in the same way. But if there were only a bottle of Spanish red 'burgundy' available to go with the fish and chips, then I would not hesitate to drink it – but I would not put any vinegar on the fried fish! There is also a certain antipathy between eggs and red wine, owing to the sulphur in eggs. But if one does not notice these things – and the human palate is very variable – there is no reason why one should observe any prohibitions.

I think it fair to add that sweet wines do not go very well with savoury dishes. This applies just as much to the great luscious German hocks as to Spanish 'sauternes'. Not only is there the sweet-sour clash but the sweet wine tends to pall after the first glass, although it is true to say that there is a small but diminishing school that supports sauternes with fish. It was popular in Edwardian days, but I cannot agree with this myself. Conversely red wines do not go well with sweet food, as they appear to be sour and bitter. It is for this reason that in France it is common to serve the cheese before the sweet or fruit. The red wine can thus be finished in comfort with a savoury course.

On one point, however, I will be dogmatic. Tobacco smoke ruins the aroma of wine and prevents one tasting it properly. In a restaurant we sometimes cannot avoid this proximity, but at home we can insist on no smoking until the meal is over. Those of us who have separate dining rooms may well be advised to prohibit smoking in that room, especially as the pungent smoke of pipes and cigars will leave an after-smell that may linger in a room for twenty-four hours or more.

These fairly simple suggestions are made in the knowledge that wine in non-wine-growing countries is something of a luxury. Every time we buy a bottle of wine we have indirectly paid a heavy duty and some freight costs on each bottle, charges which do not affect to the same degree the wine drinker in France and Italy. So, as with serving wine, to be discussed later, it is in our own interest to make sure that so far as possible we have the best out of our bottles.

In the previous chapters will have been found descriptions of most of the wines suitable for drinking with meals; so as far as possible these are not repeated here. A glance back under the appropriate wine-producing countries should supply additional information.

White Wines

It is commonly accepted that one serves dry before sweet and white before red. So first we will deal with dry white wines. The cheapest of such wines come from Spain and Portugal. The Spanish wines, as sold in Britain, tend to bear French district names, such as Spanish 'Chablis' and Spanish 'Graves'. However, under EEC rules the use of such names is now illegal. They do not really taste much like the originals, but the names give a comparative indication of style. They cost about 65p-70p. There are also white Valdepeñas and Alella at about the same price. The Portuguese whites cost about the same, but they, wisely in my view, keep their own district names or merely describe themselves as dry white, Branco Seco. A regional name is Dão, and the wine will be labelled as Dão Branco. Some dry white wine is sold as Lisbon, and under brand names, among them a dry white wine called Lagosta, bottled in a handled carafe. In my view the Portuguese wines are superior to the Spanish in the same price range.

The least expensive dry French wines are the white Mâcon (Mâcon Blanc) which come from southern Burgundy, and the white Bordeaux, sold as Bordeaux Blanc. These are in the 60p-75p class. Better in Bordeaux are the white Graves, which may be anything from a wine with just that name at 65p up to a very distinguished château-bottled wine costing £2 per bottle. Graves, even when called dry, has usually a hint of sweetness and fullness about it. There is often a suggestion of honey in the aroma. Mâcon Blanc, however, is drier and rather crisper and fresher than Bordeaux. But like all widely known generic wines, quality varies enormously. The most famous white Mâcon is Pouilly Fuissé, so-called by joining the names of the two villages whence comes some of the best of this wine. It will cost not much less than £1.20. The cheaper the more suspect, for it is a name known the world over, like the neighbouring Beaujolais, and therefore frequently misappropriated, or perhaps just badly treated. When fresh, clean with a fruity but not heavy aroma, it is an excellent wine with meals, particularly with fish. The really top Pouilly Fuissés, such as Ch. Fuissé le Clos, are every bit as good as fine single-vineyard Meursaults.

The inexpensive white burgundy that the Burgundians on the spot drink is called Aligoté, named after a grape. It is light and fresh, often a little lower in alcoholic strength than some of the finer white burgundies. It sells in the 75p-80p. range. It can be rather acid, but on the whole those imported here will be adequately full-flavoured. A reasonably dry white wine from the Bordeaux region is Entre-deux-Mers, and it is in the 60p-70p. range. It can also be slightly sweet, so it is a matter of asking your wine merchant.

One of the driest wines, especially associated with fish in general and oysters in particular, is chablis. A good many people suggest that the less good chablis includes a not-dissimilar white wine made near the mouth of the Loire, Muscadet. This is much cheaper, in the 70p-80p. class, but has not the character of a chablis. Muscadet must be bought with care, as it can be rather sharp and acid with food.

From the Loire come a variety of white wines, from the very dry to the very sweet. Rather fuller Loire white wines for drinking with meals come from lower down the river, from Saumur and Savennières, and in between there is Vouvray and its neighbour across the Loire, Montlouis.

All the drier Alsace wines make excellent dinner drinking and some will include even the Gewurztraminer and Traminer. I would exclude the more luscious of these, and certainly the Muscat.

Rather on a par with these wines are the various Rieslings made in different parts of the world, although in no case are they as good as they are in Germany. They include Yugoslavia, Hungary, Austria, Italy and South Africa. They usually are fairly cheap. A dry white Italian wine for drinking with meals is Soave, from near Verona. It costs about 85p-90p, Italian-bottled. Another is Verdicchio, rather dearer.

For drinking with meals the German wines, already described in Chapter 3, present certain problems, because many of the finest wines are certainly sweet, but not in all cases sweet enough to serve as a dessert wine. The fact that the Germans themselves often like to drink them between meals with a biscuit does not help us much, as such occasions do not seem to arise very much in the British Way of Life. Liebfraumilch has already been described, and no one can doubt that it is the most popular German white wine in Britain. As it is a blended wine it can vary very much in sweetness. I believe that for general purposes with meals the best wines are those of the

Moselle, for on the whole they are lighter than the Rhine wines, and being generally less heavy they are more suited to English food. Of these, the Saar and Ruwer wines in good years are particularly attractive for they have a good acidity level, which is not quite the same things as being acid. What is meant is that they have a good balance of sugar and acidity and so are crisp and fresh. One should choose nothing sweeter than the *Spätlese* class, and a plain village-plus-site-name wine with, for preference, Riesling added – as for example Piesporter Michelsberg Riesling – may be best, being less cloying and cheaper than the sweeter grades. There can be extremely luscious Moselles, as with the Rhine areas, but they are best avoided with savoury courses. The Nahe wines, slightly heavier than Moselles but lighter than Rhine wines, are also excellent for meals. Considering German wines here purely for suitability with savoury food, I would rank the simpler grades of Rheingau wines along with the Nahes; wines with such names as Johannisberger Klaus or Rüdesheimer. The cheapest Rhine wines are usually those from Rheinhessen – bearing such village names as Nierstein and Oppenheim – and the Palatinate, such as Hambacher and Deidesheimer. Although I would not go back on any of the suggestions already made, my broad preference for white wines with meals is certainly for those of the Côte d'Or. With plenty of flavour but unsweet they are the best wines for drinking throughout the savoury part of a meal. They can cost anything from 85p to £10 for a French domaine-bottled Montrachet, but by allowing oneself up to £1.50 some fine wines can be acquired. The list of single vineyards on page 42 may assist your choice.

On the whole the white wines of the minor Mediterranean wine-growing countries are less successful than the red. Excess of sun means too high a proportion of sugar in relation to acidity, so the wines taste flat, heavy, dull and lifeless. They tend to be fairly high in alcohol – as compared with German or Alsace wines, for example – and do not seem to me to add much to the food. There are exceptions, including some of the Austrian wines, the Slovenian white wines from the north of Yugoslavia, and sometimes the Hungarian wines. Many of them, shipped over long distances and uncertainly handled, do not show up very well by the time they reach our tables. Like the Italian, Portuguese and Spanish wines, they can be heavy and flat. They are best when bottled on the spot and shipped here, but that of course adds 10p-20p to the shop price. If price is a major consideration in preferring these wines to others, then obviously it is not worth paying the extra for foreign-bottled wine; but if you like a particular wine costing rather more, then the extra outlay is nearly always worth it in terms of enjoyment received.

Rosé Wines

If the rosé wines are best for drinking with meals, it is desirable to choose one of the firmer, drier type, such as Tavel, or one of the Jura rosés or even those from Hungary or Portugal, rather than the sweet light Anjou rosés which fade away in the mouth, and lack sufficient character to compete with any full flavoured food. Such wines are best served very cool as picnic wines. Some of the Bordeaux rosés such as Couhins, St. Agneau from the Rothschild stable, have fair character, and even the Provence and Midi rosés can have reasonable flavour. Rosé wines are the obvious answer for the occasion when it is appropriate and pleasant to serve wine, but when no one is going to pay much attention to it. It is scarcely necessary to mention the most popular of all rosés, the Portuguese Mateus Rosé.

Red Wines

The real problem of serving red wines with meals is the variety and the vintages. The latter complication does not arise with the lesser wines of the Mediterranean countries. The Spanish 'burgundies', the majority of Chiantis and the Portuguese table wines to be found in this country, are perhaps three or four years old, and intended to be drunk young. They will not as a rule improve much with age. One can drink them with enjoyment and without much concern for them or for what they are to accompany – flesh, fowl or even good red herring. They are mostly carafe wines, and they can even be mixed with a little water if too strong. They will usually improve if opened an hour or two in advance, thus removing some of their 'edges'.

When one reaches a slightly higher level, one has to decide between a fairly full, fruity wine, of which burgundy is the archetype, or a lighter wine, with which claret is typically associated. Although a red burgundy is fuller than a claret, this does not mean that it is noticeably stronger in alcohol. But there is a little more sugar in the wine and this does contribute to slightly greater alcoholic effect than claret. I have even been assured that 'there's an extra glass in a bottle of burgundy' but in fact both contain 75 centilitres, or $26^{2}/_{3}$ fluid ounces. Nevertheless, particularly for mid-day meals, I find claret less soporific than burgundy, and this is something to remember.

Among the burgundy-style wines I class those from the Rhône and from Beaujolais, Mâcon and the adjacent Mercurey and Givry, although these last four are lighter in style than Côte d'Or wines. The Loire red wines, such as Bourgueuil and Chinon, I would place on the claret side of the fence. For drinking with meals burgundy has the advantage over claret in being drinkable younger, for there is less tannin in the former wine, which gives a hard, mouth-drying taste to claret; sometimes people call this 'inky'. For mid-day drinking when subsequent duty does not call too soon or too insistently, there is much to be said for a beaujolais, and if it is a warm summer day it is a good idea to have it slightly chilled – say 58-60 degrees. It is very refreshing like that, but do not let its coolness lead you to treat it like water for thirst-quenching; it is not less alcoholic for being on the cold side. Mercureys and good red Mâcons are alternatives.

It is more than likely that most people without great experience of wine, if offered the choice of burgundy or claret would choose the former. In fact many people express surprise that claret is actually *enjoyed* rather than just a rather snobbish form of status symbol. The reason for this is that many people meet claret either too young or in restaurants where as likely as not it will be badly served as well as immature. The advantages of burgundy lie in early drinkability and a certain agreeable 'generosity', and roundness of flavour, which comes out to greet one in the bouquet. Its disadvantages are that it tends to be more expensive than modest claret and varies enormously in style. One bottle of Beaune or Nuits St. Georges may taste entirely different from other bottles bearing the same names and vintage labels, but claret usually has the advantage in price and standardization with wines bearing château names – but beware of St Julien and Médoc, which are as much liable to abuse as Beaune or Pommard. Certainly a top claret can be even more expensive than a burgundy. Although claret needs time to mature, some off-vintage wines may be very agreeable after only four years as, for example, the 1960s were by 1964. Suitable vintages are listed in Chapter 2. Another advantage of claret is its dryness, and its fruity refinement and elegance when mature.

Terms to describe wine are always open to abuse and humour, and yet not to attempt to describe them would be a confession of defeat. To call a wine 'elegant' may not convey much to the uninitiated, but the best way to decide is to open a bottle of burgundy alongside one of reasonably mature claret and see for yourself if the term fits. If not, you may be able to verbalise your own sensations.

The claret versus burgundy argument has been going on since the beginning of time, and is no more likely to be settled than the respective merits of Yorkshire and Lancashire cricket or Celtic and Rangers football. But unlike these sporting feuds the protagonists of one side or the other are always open to apparent conversion! No burgundy lover is going to refuse a proferred glass of a fine Médoc, and few Bordeaux supporters will reject a bottle of good Beaune. Both will be gratefully accepted and drunk – but the established faith on both sides is likely to be fortified as heretofore, rather than weakened!

If there is anything that red wine does go with particularly well it is cheese. And it so happens that we in Britain have some of the best cheeses in the world to accompany wine. I am not referring to Stilton, which is, like every other mature blue cheese, too strong for red or white beverage wines, but to our milder cheeses, with a good English Cheddar or Scottish Dunlop or a mature Wensleydale perhaps in the lead. The difficulty is to find them mature – which in a Cheddar probably means upwards of a year old – and not like a mixture of soap and rubber.

The superiority of English cheeses is often recognised by French wine drinkers. Not long ago a leading Bordeaux wine merchant said to me that he could not understand why Continental cheeses were so popular here when the English were so much better for wine occasions. Now to my mind French cheeses are superb, but when a Camembert or Brie is ripe and creamy it often develops a cowy, ammonia-like taste which certainly makes wine taste metallic and unpleasant.

There is much to be said, therefore, for finishing your red wine with the cheese – or, if you are having two wines, keeping your second (and it should be the better of the two) for the cheese course, which should, as in France, *precede* the sweet, after which any dry wine, red or white, will taste disagreeably sour. One wine that will stand up to Stilton or the less powerful blue cheeses is port. But it should go *with* the Stilton and not in it – a barbarous habit which converts a fine cheese into a soggy pinkish mush.

Dessert Wines
With the sweet course it must be luscious wine – a sauternes, a sweet Loire wine like Quarts de Chaume from the Coteaux du Layon, or one of the richer German wines. Another alternative is a Hungarian Tokay or one of the sweet Spanish or Portuguese white wines, although it must be recognised that these last two do not really resemble Sauternes. They are sweet but not intense in flavour as well.

Three relatively inexpensive luscious French wines to go with the sweet are the fuller types of Cérons, rich Ste Croix du Mont and very sweet Monbazillac. A white wine to go with the sweet course really has to be sweet to avoid tasting sour.

There are also unfortified red dessert wines that will stand up to sweet dishes. These include the red muscatel wines to be found around the Mediterranean, among them the unfortified type of malaga from Spain; Banyuls, from near the Mediterranean frontier between France and Spain, is a good dessert wine.

An alternative dessert wine is sweet champagne, which is very popular in France for that purpose. A dry one tastes sharp and austere with almost any pudding, but a sweet champagne, served very fresh, can be most attractive. One only needs enough for one glass a head, as it tends to cloy. Asti Spumante is another good choice here, and the many other sweet sparkling wines, previously mentioned.

8 Drinks after meals

There are four main types of after-dinner drinks: fortified wines, brandies and malt whiskies, liqueurs and eaux-de-vie, and certain types of very luscious sweet white wines.

I put fortified wines first, since the two greatest, port and madeira, can equally well be drunk at the end of a meal with uncooked fruit, such as apples, pears and bananas, or with nuts. Indeed that is how most are drunk; however it is just as agreeable to drink a bottle of fine port and madeira sitting round the fire on a winter evening. When I say a 'fine' port, I do not mean to suggest that it must necessarily be an ancient vintage port or madeira of great antiquity. A good tawny port or a rich Malmsey or Bual madeira will do excellently, but at that stage in the proceedings a ruby port or a madeira at the lower end of the price range may be rather dull-tasting, cloying and unsatisfying after the first few sips. For after-dinner drinking, and I include drinking with the fruit and nuts, the best port or madeira that you can afford should be opened. It will then come into its own. Nor has one to finish it right away, although a decanted vintage port begins to wither away in flavour after about twenty-four hours, and sooner still if kept in too warm a temperature. A tawny port lasts much better.

Madeira, that mid-Victorian mid-morning favourite, seems to me very much under-appreciated these days, as is port, though not quite to the same extent. For drinking after or at the end of a meal madeira needs to be good, and therefore fairly expensive; in the £1.75 range. The method of production already described gives a fine madeira a wonderful richness allied to a certain astringency of finish that is without parallel among wines of the world. Vintage port drinkers may not agree, but madeira, being less sweet, can be drunk a little more liberally, for that dryness in the tail delays and reduces the overwhelming fullness of vintage port; although this richness, of course, along with the great depth of flavour, is what port drinkers like.

Today, although port is not as popular as it was even a generation ago, mature vintage port is in greater demand than supply, so if one is looking for a bottle for after-dinner drinking, it may cost upwards of £2. The result of the shortage is that vintage port is being drunk too young, and such vintages as 1955, still very powerful and immature, are being drunk up. This is a pity, owing to the relative infrequency of declared port vintages. If I were asked to place post-war vintages in order of drinking date, my list would be as follows: 1950, 1947, 1954 (only declared by one or two shippers), 1958, 1960, 1955, 1948, 1963, 1966. It is understood, I hope, that I am not suggesting knocking off the neck of a bottle of 1963 port if there is nothing else to hand! The 1950 may be drunk now, the others in succession, and the 1966 in or beyond about 1980.

Faced with the vintage port shortage, one or two shippers have shipped possible alternatives: a late-bottled vintage wine. A traditional alternative is crusted port, which is a blended port of more than one vintage, but laid down in bottle for a long period. Rather rare these days, it is often very good indeed, and less appreciated than it might be.

An obvious dessert wine is a fine Oloroso sherry, of which the so-called cream sherries are today the most popular. This term arose indirectly from the rich type of sherry known for over 300 years as Bristol Milk, associated with the West-Country city and port, and naturally sold by the leading Bristol wine merchants, including Harveys and Averys. It was the former who produced an even richer version and called it Bristol Cream, a protected trade mark. It has now been followed by many other cream sherries, such as Armada Cream and Celebration Cream.

To be good these cream sherries must not be merely sweet; they should contain a high proportion of really old sherries, of twenty-five to fifty years old. I remember a merchant of one of the sherries, not very long after the last war, being faced by an American customer, indignant that he could not secure all he required. It was hard to explain to him that it was not possible to increase at will the amount of fifty-year-old sherry in the blend! These cream sherries are not, of course, the only rich sherries and other fine Olorosos may be just as good. But as with port and madeira, dessert sherries should have the subtlety which only age and maturity can give. There are also the Cyprus 'cream' sherries, which in their price range are not all bad accompaniments to nuts.

Before leaving sweet fortified wines, for these occasions, one must mention marsala and the fortified type of malaga, although the former is more often opened in the kitchen than in the living room, and malaga is little imported into Britain. I have tasted marsalas lacking in 'follow-through' in the flavour, but a fine old vergine marsala is not unlike a good madeira, but lighter.

It is a matter of taste, but an opinion poll among after-dinner drinkers would probably place brandy at the top of the list. After a good and probably substantial meal, brandy produces an astringent and cleansing effect on the palate, and in not too large quantities it 'settles the stomach', to use an old-fashioned phrase.

There is perhaps more unnecessary 'mystique' about brandy than about any other drink, and in the past at least the advertising of the leading cognac firms has cumulatively contributed to an impression of a rather snob drink, although until recently the price of three star brandy was not appreciably higher than whisky, which in Britain at least has never carried the social overtones of brandy. In France, on the other hand, it is the whisky that carries the overtones, while the ordinary workman will readily have his glass of *'fine'* at his local café.

To many people brandy seems 'difficult' owing to the star and letter system of labelling (now on the decline), and to uncertainty as to what to look for when making the considerable outlay that brandy, like all spirits, entails. Then arises the question of serving in 'correct' glasses, the temperature, and so on.

Owing to the disproportionately high duty, the more you pay, within reason, the better the brandy in the bottle. Consequently for after-dinner drinking the VSOP quality of brandy costing £1 or so more a bottle than the normal three-star – is usually well worth the extra. In most cases this is also true with the higher grades of cognac. There is a much larger proportion of really old brandies in them. It is unnecessary nowadays, I hope, to warn against the ancient- looking, cobwebbed bottle and the 'Napoleon brandy'. Brandy does not improve in bottle, and after twenty years or so may well begin to deteriorate, as well as to rot the cork. Some people think that a good deep colour in a brandy is a recommendation, but it can be the other way round. Hence in the initials VSOP – the 'P' stands for 'pale'. Perhaps I am influenced by the fact that what I regard as the finest cognac of all is usually very pale; in Chapter I have already advertised the merits of early-landed vintage cognac.

The choice of brandy will to some extent depend on individual taste, for the great firms certainly have a 'house style'. Martell is to my way of thinking smoother than Hennessy, which is more vigorous and full-flavoured; so is Hine but softer; Denis Mounié and Delamain are light in colour and delicate. Salignac is perhaps midway between.

The old markings of quality such as Three Star and VSOP have tended to break down in recent years. So Hennessy, who are said to have invented the system, have changed their Three Star into Bras Armé, Martell go in for Cordon Bleu and Cordon Argent, Delamain have a Pale and Dry, while Salignac's finer quality is Napoleon, without pretending that it derives from the imperial cellar.

Armagnac is an alternative to cognac, and the star letter system is used there too. As it tends to be rather more pungent than cognac it is certainly worth having the VSOP and better qualities. There are those who assert that armagnac is less 'mucked about' than much cognac, and certainly it is worth trying. Among the brands to be found in Britain are Janneau, Marquis de Caussade, Marquis de Montesquiou and Kressman.

Many people think that the most satisfactory after-meal drinks are eaux-de-vie, referred to on pages 26 and 60. The French often call them *'digestifs'*, and of course they are 'straight', unsweetened, and with a certain 'cut' in their flavour which may well do one good after a large meal. Kirsch is the best known, Kümmel is popular, and I have found the pear eau-de-vie, usually known as Poire William, often a little softer than some of the others. Frequently however, they are bottled far too early and so are hard, even harsh. Calvados or applejack is in the same class, and I have seldom found one that was not far too powerful and immature, although Trou Normand is palatable. From Central Europe come the popular peach, plum and apricot brandies, and they can be very good – if old enough.

So far as unfortified wines are concerned, the best after-dinner wines are surely the rich, luscious German wines from the Moselle, Nahe and the Rhine – and a few from Franconia. Even if one can afford them one does not have to go as far as the wonderfully rich and usually extremely expensive *beerenauslese* and *trocken-beerenauslese* wines, costing anything from £3.50 to over £10 a bottle. These are wonderful wines for drinking on their own, as they have a residual freshness, arising from a perfect balance of sugar and acidity, which prevents them from being cloying, as may be the case with even a fine sauternes. But the less exalted categories, the *spätlese* and *auslese* wines, can be admirable for drinking without food. They are often too sweet for savoury food and not quite sweet enough even for fresh fruit. A bottle served fresh and cool will go round six or seven people. Although seemingly a little foreign to our way of entertaining, to invite a few friends in to drink a fine bottle of German wine is a very pleasant way of spending an evening.

9 How to serve wine

High up on the list of wine myths is the nonsense talked about serving wine, the 'correct' glasses, the 'right' temperature and so on, allied to 'gracious living' and the like. All this has produced a natural reaction, and to combat wine-snobbery there is the slosh-it-into-the-tumbler school. As with most other things connected with wine, there is some sense behind the nonsense; but it must not be elevated into a ritual. These guides to the enjoyment of wine are means to an end, not ends in themselves.

It is worth establishing that wine does respond to good or bad treatment and that most wine will taste better or worse according to the way it is handled in the home.

Take first the question of temperature. It is generally agreed that a red wine tastes best when it is at what is commonly called room temperature. As most British houses are on the cold side, while American houses are often too warm, it is safer to say that a red wine will taste at its best at a temperature between about 65 degrees F. and not more than 70 degrees F. If too cold it is numb and tends to taste hard and bitter; if too warm it loses its aroma and tastes flabby or even vinegary. Broadly speaking, fine wines should not be served at open-air meals, for then they are usually too cold or too warm, and their aroma is dissipated.

On the other hand, a white wine should taste fresh and cool, and the sweeter the wine, the cooler it should be when served. For a warm white wine tastes flabby, flat and mawkish; if at all sweet it will taste cloying; warm sparkling wine in particular tastes awful. A good temperature for a dry white wine is about 50 to 55 degrees; champagne and really sweet wine can well be 5 degrees cooler.

Most of us will cool our wine in a refrigerator. Assuming that it is moderately but not very cold, about 45 minutes should 'freshen' a dry white wine, about 60 minutes for sparkling wine, and up to 90 minutes for a really luscious sweet wine. For dry sherry rather over 30 minutes should make sure it is 'crisp'.

Dry sherry, dry madeira and white or aperitif port will certainly taste crisper and fresher if served cool; warm sherry, as it is all too often served in restaurants and pubs, is limp, losing that freshness that is desirable for all aperitifs. On the other hand the sweet sherries should be served at room temperature, as with port and the sweeter madeiras. The dividing line for sherry is at the Amontillado level.

This should be served cool; the Olorosos, Brown and Cream sherries at normal red wine temperature. In summer the borderline wines for chilling, such as dry madeira, are more enjoyable when fresh; in winter a Sercial may be served at room temperature.

With cognac the question of temperature brings out the chi-chi, for it is associated with the type and size of glass.

There are no 'rules' about what glasses to use for various types of wine, but the wine will smell and taste better if certain simple conditions are observed. First, the glass should be large rather than small, for a wine develops its aroma and flavour better in a receptacle allowing a fair amount of the wine to be in direct contact with the air. Far better a good size tumbler than one of those tiny glasses commonly, and unsuitably, used for liqueurs. Secondly, the wine will be tasted more easily if the glass is not too thick, for the wine flows more easily into the mouth. In certain circles there is a certain snobbism for drinking champagne in tankards; absorbed across a thick silver or pewter lip, it never tastes the same to me. Also, of course, one of the pleasures of wine is to see the colour; then it can tell one something about the wine and its condition. Thirdly, it does help the rather delicate aroma of wine, if the glass is narrow at the top compared with the maximum width of the bowl. This is, of course, the idea behind the balloon glass, and in Burgundy it is common to find the local red wines served in moderate-sized balloon glasses. There too you will find gold-fish bowls on long stalks, but these are generally for the impressionable tourist. I myself have had pleasure at Beaune in waving away large near-spheres, and insisting on reasonable sized glasses more suitable for the dining room than the aquarium.

Finally, glasses should be clear in colour so that the wine can be seen. The old-fashioned German wine glasses – green for Moselle and brown for Rhine wines – were designed to hide impurities in the wine. These impurities have now been eliminated by modern wine production methods, so it is unnecessary to obscure anything in coloured glasses. For the same reason, plain glasses are much to be

---

opposite:
Glasses are specially designed for different wines and spirits. Wine and brandy glasses are shaped to show colour and to cup the aroma.
Top row: (from left): Burgundy - champagne - sherry (dock glass) - various - Martini - claret
Lower row: Champagne flute - port - Highball - old fashioned - German wines - Brandy

preferred to cut glasses, elegant though these may look; of course the stem and the foot may be cut. The reason why glasses have stems, and German wine glasses tend to have very long stems, is, for white wines in particular, so that the wine is not warmed by the hand round the bowl. This does not apply so readily to red wine, but all wine looks better in a stemmed glass.

There is no reason to have different styles or sizes of glass for different wines. A large, all-purpose one is quite good enough, and it will do for sparkling wines and port as well as for tables wines. It is traditional for vintage port to be served in rather small glasses filled to the brim, but for reasons already explained this dissipates the aroma; because a large glass is used, it does not mean that one has to pour more into it.

Some people believe that champagne should be served in the flat, saucer-shaped glass known as a 'coupe'. This is not, as some people believe, the traditional shape, and no one in the wine trade in Champagne itself would think of using a glass of this type. Champagne is the one wine which requires minimal contact with the air, for the wider the surface exposed, the quicker the bubbles of gas will come to the surface and the sooner the wine will become flat. Champagne is best served in the slightly incurving narrow glass illustrated. An alternative is the flute, also shown on page 128.

One of the snobbisms associated with brandy is the big balloon glass. This may satisfy the self-esteem of tycoons, but is a vulgarism. The idea behind it, to concentrate the aroma at the top of the glass, is sound enough, and there is no objection to a small balloon glass. Personally I prefer a thistle shape, which has the same effect. But any incurving wine glass will do, or those slightly conical dock glasses, as shown on page 128.

The argument against a large glass for brandy, is that the brandy is improved by being slightly warmed, for this brings out the aroma. This warming should be done by the hand and *not* by artificial heat, as may occasionally be seen in restaurants, when the wine waiter with a great show warms the large balloon over the flame of the spirit lamp. Result – the glass smells of methylated spirit, and is so warm that the volatile spirit in the brandy begins to evaporate!

It is desirable that wine glasses should be fairly thin. To the objection that this implies fragility and breakages, my reply is that wine glasses should be washed up the morning after! No soap, soap powder or detergent should be used; only hot water and a clean linen towel. The glasses should be stored standing up to avoid picking up any aroma from a cupboard shelf: a glass, clean but odorous, can ruin the aroma of a wine. This may seem rather a fine point to some people, but apart from the pleasure of smelling a wine, it is the nose that will probably give the first warning if there is something wrong with a wine. A white wine smelling excessively of sulphur – put in quite legitimately in correct proportions to stop the wine fermenting in the bottle and to keep it fresh – will not taste very agreeable, nor will a red wine if it has either a woody, corky or vinegary smell.

The question of a corky wine often arouses discussion. It is not always easy to be sure that a wine is corky, although, if affected, the longer it is left open to the air, the fouler it will smell. Quite often a bottle of wine, particularly an oldish one, will not smell very pleasant immediately after the cork is drawn. This is known as 'bottle stink', and if the wine is sound it will pass in a matter of minutes. A 'corked' or 'corky' wine is a different matter. This arises from a fungus in the cork itself, and the wine picks up a distinct smell and taste of cork. There are degrees and stages of this, and that is why it is sometimes difficult to tell whether or not a wine is corked. But anyone who has smelled and tasted a really 'corky' bottle will have no doubt about it. A piece of cork in the wine does no harm at all for, after all, the wine is in contact with the cork when the bottle is laid on its side, as all table wine should be for keeping purposes.

The next matter is uncorking the bottle. There are many types of corkscrew on the market. I favour one with a rather broad, wide screw, as the gimlet type is liable to pull through an old cork. All too many corkscrews, including many of the types used by waiters, have too short a screw, with the result that it may not penetrate the length of the cork, and so break it off in the neck of the bottle. This is a nuisance, but, as just mentioned, the wine will not be harmed by some cork fragments if it is impossible to remove the remainder before pouring the wine out. The corkscrew should be applied to the middle of the top of the cork, although diagonal insertion may be an advantage if the cork is likely to be difficult to extract, as in vintage port or old table wines. So far as possible the bottle should be held steady and not revolved, so that if there is any sediment down at the bottom it will be disturbed as little as possible. A good strong steady pull is all that is required. As just indicated, the most difficult type of cork to draw is without a doubt that of an old bottle of vintage port. Owing to the action of the spirit in the wine, the cork usually disintegrates. For such wines the old-fashioned lattice-work corkscrews have most effective traction power. There is also a technique of knocking off the neck of a bottle with a glancing blow from the handle of a large knife, but some instruction from a skilled wine merchant is best for this drastic method, and then some practice, preferably out of doors!

This brings one to decanting. Does it improve the wine or not? Is it just part of the snobbery of wine?

For white wines and inexpensive red wines of the Spanish 'burgundy' variety it is not necessary. The principal reason for decanting is to take the wine off the sediment, so that everyone sharing the wine has perfectly clear wine; the sediment also has a sourish taste. Very few white wines have any sediment at all, although sometimes one sees some crystals or a little brown sandy deposit at the bottom of the bottle; so only in exceptional cases is decanting necessary. Incidentally, no one should be put off a bottle of white wine with a little deposit in it; there is unlikely to be anything wrong with the wine itself.

On the other hand nearly all wine benefits from being opened a little time before it is drunk. The coarser and rougher the wine, the more it may benefit and soften down from exposure to the air. Half an hour should be long enough. The general rule is that the older the wine, the less time it should be given to 'breathe'; for if it is a bit 'weak at the knees' it will certainly not stand much oxydation. But a fine ten-year-old red wine will almost certainly improve by having an hour or so to mingle a little with the air. Then there are some port drinkers who maintain that a fine vintage port tastes better the day following the opening. The easiest way to achieve aeration is to pour the wine out of its original bottle into another receptacle – to decant it, in fact. One does not need to have a glass decanter for the purpose, although the wine will look agreeable in one, especially if the decanter is not over-cut or too much decorated. Alternatively, the obvious temporary resting place for the wine is another bottle, so long as it is thoroughly clean. A jug, even a large enough milk bottle, will do at a pinch.

Some people are put off decanting by pictures of venerable bottles being held over candles, but this is all nonsense. If there is sediment in a wine, obviously it should be left behind in the bottle. Bottle-glass is dark for a very good reason: light bleaches a red wine. Vintage port is in black bottles, for traditionally the wine is likely to lie for a long time. So, to make sure that the sediment does not enter the decanted wine, a light is necessary in order to see inside the bottle. A table lamp or a pocket torch placed under the bottle is much more effective than a candle, which throws a weak light only. If one puts a candle too near the glass, then the latter may suddenly become very hot from the naked flame. Then, after wiping the lip of the bottle over which the wine will flow, one takes up the bottle, label upwards (for the bottle should be lying that way up and any sediment will, therefore, be on the lower side), and, holding it near the base, pours steadily, without stopping, into the receptacle. Do not pour too fast, for then the air bubbles may disturb the sediment. When the sediment reaches the neck, stop – and use the residue for cooking. The wine itself should be bright. The decanter stopper should be left out, except for very old wine.

When one pours out the wine the glass should not be filled more than about half way, for then one can swill it around in the glass, thus giving the air a chance to reach as much of the wine as possible, and so release the aroma. For some reason it is traditional in places like colleges and messes to pour vintage port right up to the level of the rim of a small glass. I suspect the idea is that thus everyone has the same ration on each round of the port decanter. But it is far better for the sake of the wine to pour the same quantity into a larger glass.

One of the problems that we all meet is, how much wine does one need for a given number of people. The late Maurice Healy, KC, remarked that in London his ration was half a bottle, in Paris a bottle, but in Bordeaux he could drink two bottles! But then he was a very practised drinker, and a great deal depends on how accustomed one's guests are to drinking wine. This is as much a matter of habit as of alcoholic capacity. I have known dinner parties where two bottles sufficed for fourteen people – the glasses were very small; the company very wine-shy! For many people one glass will last them through the meal. There are $26^2/_3$ ounces in the average wine bottle, and allowing for wastage with red wines, there should be at least 24 ounces available, and more of white wine. A three-ounce measure is reasonable, although a four-ounce one is more generous; for the latter you need a fairly large glass, as specified earlier, if it is not to be over-full. So a bottle will serve six or eight people with one glass a head. I think that for ordinary purposes at least one bottle for three people should be reckoned on, while I would confess to preferring a half bottle a head. It depends, of course, on what one drinks beforehand, and even afterwards. It also depends on the occasion and the time of day.

In the order of serving wines, the general rule is to serve white before red wine and dry before sweet. This is sound practice, except that a dry red wine – and most are dry – should precede a sweet white one. A sweetish German wine, for example, will kill a claret or burgundy that may follow it, for these will seem sour.

Some people are afraid of serving a variety of wines at a meal, on the grounds that mixing drinks may have unfortunate effects. So far as the alcoholic content is concerned, there is no cause for alarm; but, obviously, any excess of rather rich drinks, such as Sauternes or port, piled on top of perhaps rather rich food, will not be received kindly by the stomach. It is certainly better to drink all wines with some accompaniment, especially sparkling wines. For the 'gas' goes quickly into the blood stream, and the effects can be felt very quickly; food delays this.

One point which perplexes many people is the order of serving vintage wines. In my view the soundest principle is to serve the youngest first and then by ascending seniority. A vigorous young red wine will not, for example, kill an older one if the latter is sound. Rather the more mature, well-balanced, older wine will make the young wine unattractive and out-of-place. If, say, an old wine is showing its age and would show unfavourably when served second after an exceptionally full-bodied wine – a 1950 claret after the abnormally fruity 1961 – then do not serve the two wines on the same occasion.

Of course seniority is not a consideration when white and red wines are being served at the same meal, i.e. one can serve a 1966 white burgundy and then a 1967 claret.

It is seldom a good idea to serve claret and red burgundy together. The claret will taste too thin, the burgundy too obvious. True, they do it in France at official banquets, but then we serve wine better in Britain.

All the words written about wine are but a prelude or an accompaniment to drinking. It is hoped that the necessarily concise comments in this small book on the enormous variety of wines and spirits available to us will have served not only as explanation but as encouragement. For wine drinking is among the most agreeable and, in moderation, most innocent pleasures that we can give ourselves and our friends. We can drink like millionaires at pounds a bottle or much more modestly for less than a single pound; and round the corner or within reach of a letter there are always unknown wines, fresh vintages, new experiences to be found. Good drinking!

Index